SHAMANISM
And Sacred Landscapes

Chris Trwoga

Anne Kirkbride
Oct 06.

Shamanism And Sacred Landscapes © 2006 Chris Trwoga
All rights reserved.

No part of this book may be used or reproduced in any form
without written permission from the author except in the case
of quotations in articles and reviews.

Front cover illustrations and collages © Lloyd Drew 2006
Photographs of Avebury on pages 102 & 120 © Lloyd Drew 2006
Seahenge images pages 41 & 42 by Mark Brennand & Jason Dawson,
courtesy of Norfolk Museums & Archaeology Service.
All other photographs © Chris Trwoga 2006

Published by:
The Speaking Tree
5, High Street
Glastonbury
Somerset BA6 9DP
01458 831800

www.speakingtree.co.uk

Layout & design by Lloyd Drew, Sanctum Arts,
Glastonbury 01458 830814

ISBN: 0953674533

Contents

Part One: Towards a Philosophy of Shamanism — 4

    Prelude 4
1.1   Shamanism and Science – Opening our Eyes to the Sacred 9
1.2.   A Trip to the Movies – The Nature of Shamanic Ecstasy 14
1.3.   Earth and Humanity – The Function of Myth in Shamanic Experiences 24

Part Two: Shamanism and Sacred Landscapes — 29

2.1.   The Spiritual Orphan – The Significance of Landscape in Shamanic Culture 29
2.2.   Remythologizing the Earth – Understanding the Importance of Place 32
2.3.   Sacred Landscapes – The Problem of Relationships and Identity 37
2.4.   Exploring Inner Landscapes – Carl Jung and the Psychology of Shamanism 43

Part Three: Interpreting Shamanic Landscapes — 57

    Preface – Reading the Monuments 57
3.1.   Shamanic Maps 59
3.2.   Shamanism and British Prehistory – The Mesolithic Age 61
3.3.   Shamanism and Landscapes Today – Comparisons with the Khanty of Siberia 66
3.4.   Houses for the Dead – The Earthen Long Barrow 71
3.5.   Feasts for the Living and the Dead – Causewayed Enclosures 77
3.6.   Gateways to the Underworld – Megaliths and Passage Graves 78
3.7.   The Shaman's Key – The Rock Carvings of Ancient Britain 85
3.8.   Stone Circles, Standing Stones, Wood Henges and the Concept of the Cosmic Tree 92
3.9.   Spirit Paths – Cursus Monuments 97
3.10. The Beginning of the End – Bronze Age Round Barrows 98
    Conclusion 100

Part Four: Five Shamanic Landscapes — 103

    Introduction 103
4.1.   In the Shadow of the First Stonehenge – St. David's, Pembrokeshire 105
4.2.   Shamans of a Lost Kingdom – Avebury 119
4.3.   The Valley of Ghosts – Kilmartin Glen 135
4.4.   Spirits of the Stone – The Peak District 147
4.5.   The Twilight of the Shaman - Dartmoor 159

References: — 168

Prelude

Unlike the others, I did not dress the part.
We sat in a tipi, under a Somerset sky,
Beating drums and burning sage,
Aping the rituals of dead men in feathers.

The terror came from my own grandfathers,
Whose dust I profaned by neglect.
They overwhelmed me from the ordinary dirt
And whilst I slept they ate my soul.

SHAMANISM IS OUR OLDEST surviving expression of human spirituality. It is rooted in the belief that all that exists has a spirit or soul. Shamanism explores inner realities, opening the doors of perception by altering the experiences of the body. According to Carl Jung, one of the giants of twentieth century psychology, shamanism taps into the subconscious mind, connecting us to those same spiritual experiences, or archetypes, that shaped the evolution of our hominid ancestors. To use shamanism to explore the possibilities for spiritual growth is to begin at the beginning. It is to explore human spirituality before cults and creeds and the Age of Priesthood. It demands of the scientific materialist that they rethink the arid mantra that only the visible world exists.

Unlike Religion and Scientific Materialism, Shamanism does not offer a framework through which we must see the world. Rather, it demands that every man must learn to see with his own eyes. Shamanism is based on raw, human experience and the interpretation of those experiences lies with the shaman and his immediate community.

Carl Jung insisted that every man should be his own shaman. To do this we must develop the psychological anchors that will enable us to weather the storms of self-realization in a world where everything conspires to conformity. I believe that the way of the shaman opens the door to rediscovering what we are and what our relationship with the earth should be.

I humbly offer you my own journey to rediscover the shamans of my ancestors.

What is a Shaman?

The defining characteristic of the shaman is his ability to enter a trance state, or 'ecstasy', in which he travels to the Otherworld – the world of the spirit – to do business on behalf of his community. That business may be to escort a spirit of someone who has recently died, rescue the soul of a sick man from the spirit who stole it, or fend off attacks from demonic forces that are attacking his entire community. He identifies the spirits that are causing harm and uses his powers to redirect their energies away from those he seeks to protect. The shaman does

Prelude

his work in the realms of the unconscious, passing through the gate to the Otherworld through trance or the use of hallucinogenic drugs.

The shaman brings healing by mediating with spirit forces - be they benign or malevolent - which threaten his community. He understands that individuals and communities become dislocated from their true nature, causing disharmony in their relationship with the world and each other. The shaman's role is to be a man of his time, identifying the hurt in his community and bringing healing and reconciliation. A good shaman does this with consummate skill, bending reality with words and changing the shape of the past to forge an anchor for a better future. The shaman knows what lies in our unconscious and is able to reconcile history and myth to create new beginnings. As with the shaman of the Rainforest and the Australian outback, the modern shaman's ability to heal stems from his own belief in *anima*, or spirits, and the belief of others in his power to appease or control them.

The shaman is found amongst the primitive hunter-gatherer communities of the world and wherever Western thought and religion has not done its damage. He is, along with the way of the hunter, as old as humanity. It is possible that a million years ago archaic man danced and shamanized around their campfires in the Ethiopian savanna. Traces of their visions survive in the painted bison and strange winged men of the caves at Lascaux, created when Britain was still buried under ice. In Australia, they are part of a living culture that goes back 50,000 years.

19th century engraving of Siberian shaman from 'Moeurs et costumes de la Russie'

The short period of human history that separates modern western society from the time of the shaman has changed our lifestyles and surroundings, but has done nothing to change the fundamental needs, urges, and emotions of the human psyche. A thin veneer of technology distances us from the people of the Lower Paleolithic – no more – and technology has little to offer when the storms of a spiritual crisis threaten to overwhelm us.

The experiences that create the shaman are well documented. They focus on a night of terror in which the initiate is dismembered by invisible forces and then brought back to life by the spirits who have devoured his flesh and blood. The community to which the shaman belongs may subject the young man or woman to secret ordeals, which bring the spiritual crisis to a head. The shaman is restored to life, strong, transformed, and with the power to do business with the spirits of the living and the dead. A profound, life-changing experience – symbolized by the shaman's 'night of terror' - can strike anyone at any time. Adaptation – the re-defining of who we are – is essential

Shamanism and Sacred Landscapes

Prelude

if we are to survive. It applies to individuals, it applies to communities, and it applies to the planet. The power needed to turn our lives around when everything is falling apart is the same for us as it is for the shaman.

If you are prepared to experience that 'dark night of the soul' in which you will be torn apart by psychic forces then the rewards can be immeasurable. The shaman is restored with bones and joints of iron that will not yield again.

The Shaman's World

"Every real shaman has to feel an illumination in his body, in the inside of his head or in his brain, something that gleams like fire, that gives him the power to see with closed eyes in the darkness, into the hidden things or into the future, or into the secrets of another man." Arctic shaman. [1]

We live out our lives in two landscapes. The first landscape is that of our conscious, waking life, in which our experiences are shaped by our education, our upbringing, and the values and beliefs of the times we live in. It is the world of solidity, of material things, of money, possessions, and the daily grind. It is the world of the television, the Internet and the ephemeral heroes of the mass media. In medieval times it was called the world of the 'profane'.

The second landscape is as old as life itself. Formed over countless generations, our brains and central nervous systems contain the Realm of the Unconscious - and it is a world rich beyond imagining. This world expresses itself in our dreams and deepest felt desires. In it we may travel free from our bodies and speak once more with the dead. Carl Jung identified this landscape as the *collective unconscious* – inherited memories and experiences, buried in the subconscious, but influencing our lives profoundly. The *archetypes* out of which our experiences in this landscape are constructed have been with us since the first manifestations of human thought.

In primitive language, it is the realm of the ancestors and of animal spirits. It is also the world of the demon – the destructive side of our psyche - that Jung referred to as 'the shadow'. These constitute our collective spiritual inheritance and are as real, in experiential terms, as the physical world. When Australian Aborigines describe this world of ancestral spirits as the 'Dreamtime', when their remote ancestors took the form of animals, they are describing a truth uncontested by modern science. The Realm of the Unconscious was forming even as we left the primordial seas and evolved to breathe the air. The shaman enters this most ancient of landscapes to bring about change – for good or evil – by bringing the archetypal forces of the unconscious to bear on our waking, rational world. We call this landscape 'the sacred'. The landscape of the sacred lies above and below the profane world of our daily lives.

Prelude

In shamanic cosmology, these dimensions are perceived as being connected by an axis – often symbolized by the Cosmic Tree. The shaman ascends this Tree in order to travel between the different psychic realms. The axis passes, symbolically, through a hole, or opening, which is nothing less than a stairway between the worlds.

To walk unharmed in the Realms of the Unconscious is not easy. It is, for some, the path to madness. The unwary risk psychic destruction. Primitive communities chose men and women to become shamans who had shown themselves strong in the face of the dangers of the spirit world. They had experienced being torn apart by demonic forces and survived. They had died and, having seen the faces of the gods, returned healed. Physical and mental stamina of an extraordinary kind had to be demonstrated before a man or woman could be initiated into the shaman's mysteries.

The mythologies, landscapes, traditions, and taboos of his community shape the shaman's world. He keeps his community in balance, underpinning the realities of soul, spirit, and ancestors in a dangerous world where his power is needed to combat the darkness. His experiences are an affirmation of the wisdom and mythology, the totems and taboos of generations past. He shamanizes in public, often before his entire community. It is sacred theatre in which he performs both for his living audience and for the spirit forces that only he can see.

Our studies of the shaman have not helped us to understand his world. We may describe what we see – we may even try to emulate him – but it is very difficult to follow the shaman's path to the Unseen Realm. We may take the same psychedelic drugs as the shaman, or drum and dance until we attain ecstasy, but the world we enter is fractured by our lack of understanding and belief. We no longer have the experiential grounding to be where he is. We can't just assume the mind-set of a nineteenth century Native American or Australian Aborigine. Our intellectual lumber-rooms are too cluttered to ingest the purity of their myth and the immediacy of their gods and spirits. Science and technology have driven the ghost out of the machine.

The shaman's own world is in retreat. As money, alcohol, TV, Coca Cola and commercial exploitation eat into the cultures of native peoples around the world, the true shamans are losing ground in their own communities. They have become an oddity, a curiosity among the smiling people of the rainforest, who now display their most sacred and secret acts before our cameras. In the age of ongoing medical advances, technological development, and the psychotherapist's couch, the shaman has become a sideshow for academics and cranks. They were once our spiritual tigers, and, like the tiger, they are now threatened with extinction as their cultural and intellectual habitats are destroyed.

Part 1:
Towards a Philosophy of Shamanism

1.1. Shamanism and Science
Opening our eyes to the Sacred

"If we are to judge the future by the past, our present way of looking at the world, natural and correct as it seems to us, is probably only transitional and will perhaps one day appear as remote, absurd, and unnatural to our descendents as the worst extravagance of savage opinion now appears to us."

J.G. Frazer, in a letter to Henry Jackson, 1888.

"Our age has shifted all emphasis to the here and now, and thus brought about a daimonisation of man and his world. The phenomenon of dictators and all the misery they have wrought springs from the fact that man has been robbed of transcendence by the short-sightedness of the super-intellectuals."

Carl Jung

SCIENCE BANISHED THE GODS and spirits from the temples and mountain-tops and exiled them to the realms of children's storybooks. We cannot see the Soul, therefore, that which is our essential self cannot be properly said to exist. Some have even used science to explain away shamanism itself. Timothy Leary attempted to replicate the shaman's experiences using hallucinogenic drugs. Others have argued that the shaman's world is constructed out of 'entoptic phenomena' - the name given to the shapes and patterns generated in the retina when we enter a trance state. Shamanic 'flight' can be replicated using drugs, magnetic fields, or specific sound frequencies. Some Psychologists have defined the various kinds of shamanic experience as grounded in one kind of mental illness or another.

Some try to recover that understanding by replicating the environment of the shaman, using tipis, smudges, feathers, drums, costume and the entire paraphernalia of a lost culture. This does not even have the 'respectability' of scientific research and for me is a kind of shamanic 'Black and White Minstrel Show'. If I replicate what I see the Native American doing, the modern shaman argues, then this must be shamanizing. It is not. Shamanism is a way of seeing. The entire wardrobe, tool-kit, and environment of the shaman do no more than facilitate the shamanic experience. The props are not important. What is important is their symbolic value and our understanding of the spiritual landscapes they represent.

Towards a Philosophy of Shamanism

Underpinning the shamanic vision is a philosophy of being which cannot be explored by 'scientific' means. It affirms that the world of the spirit is more real than the world of flesh and bone. It affirms that the spirit drives the visible world and without it, the entire material process would vanish away. Science is searching for the *why* of the physical world. Why does *b* follow *a*? Shamanism has identified the *why* as being an immense web of psycho-spiritual beings or souls, which energize all things. The shaman's technology strives to control and harness this power through visionary experiences.

Stephen Larsen aptly describes the limitations of the scientist in dealing with matters of shamanism and the soul:

"The scientist is only the magician of the daylight world. He has lost touch with the nocturnal world of the imagination, where self-luminous forms and beings dwell and where the mind participates in constructing the universe it perceives. He is only in touch with his abstract logic or his experimental design, and is thus an exile from the mythological; his magic belongs to the universe seen only in one specialized state of consciousness." [2]

Valid scientific research needs an objective basis. This inevitably reduces all our experiences to *brain states*. If I stub my toe the *experience* of pain is a brain state and hence is a phenomenon of neural activity within my skull, which the scientist *can* study and report on. But this is not my experience of pain. The experience, and hence the *consciousness* of pain, is in my toe and I alone have that experience. It is a common for amputees to continue to experience pain in the amputated limb. Pain, in other words, can be *experienced* in empty space. Brain activity may indeed be generating the sensation of pain. The *experience*, however, is in the foot that is no longer there. How much further can our experiences be projected? Thousands of people have had *out of body* experiences. The car racer feels the very contact of the tyre with the road. The person dying from a heart attack experiences travelling down a tunnel of light. We do not have to understand the mechanics of extended or projected consciousness. All we have to do in order to begin the quest for shamanic power is to affirm the reality of such experiences alongside the reality of all other experiences. The followers of Jesus *experienced* the reality of His resurrection (the ultimate shamanic trick) and that is all the entire edifice of Christianity has to go on.

Where does all of this take us?

It takes us to the primacy of the conscious experience and the existential reality of the things that I experience. Spirits and demons may be as real for me as they were for the medieval mind. Shamanic journeying might be part of my world, as it was for the shaman of old. We shape our own reality and our crude 'scientific' world-view has made us blind to the immense potential of the Universe of the Imagination. The experienced world *is real* because it is the only universe you and I can ever inhabit.

Towards a Philosophy of Shamanism

Who closed the doorway of our imagination, leaving our wings clipped and denying us access to the gods?

Before the advent of the Scientific Age, the orthodoxy of the Church had gone a long way toward undermining the primacy of human experience. As societies became more settled and complex, the priesthood usually assumed the role of interpreting the mythic world for the layman, telling him *how the world is*. Orthodoxy (a fixed view of the world) was created in the form of sacred texts and a fixed mythology, which became the vehicle for validating religious experiences. The shaman, the prophet, and the seer are pushed to the edges of such societies, often to the point of persecution. Once we had the Ten Commandments, we no longer need Moses or the mountain. The heretic is a heretic because he sees things differently. He has kept his eyes open when others see only what is written on tablets of stone.

We have a new orthodoxy now. It is called Science. Science has stripped the emperor of his clothes and we all know he is naked. We can no longer be fooled into believing in things that we cannot see. And yet all great scientific advances are born out of the dreams and visions of great men. Scientists do create new worlds. It is the masses that have made a god of Science and think that Science, like Yahweh, writes on tablets of stone.

The New Age phenomenon has engendered a fascination with things mysterious. Those coming to shamanism, Eastern spiritual practices and so-called 'earth mysteries' from the modern western tradition often find it difficult, sometimes impossible ,to see *things differently*. They see everything through the filter of 'scientific' thinking. The result is a crude, populist understanding of both the soul and science. Books on Feng Shui, on crystal healing, ley-lines, prehistoric monuments, the pyramids – the list is endless - all use a pseudo-scientific language. Stonehenge is measured for its energy lines, its megalithic yard, and its astronomical accuracy. Sound measuring equipment, magnetometers, and surveying equipment are dragged round our sacred sites in order to make sense of the megalithic mind. Archaeologists dissect the tombs of the ancestors and describe their findings in meaningless lists of assemblages. The experience of what Rudolf Otto called the *Mysterium Tremendum* is now entirely described according to the new 'scientific' world-view.

The populist view of science and its interpretation of reality has done more than empty our churches. It has stripped the *Mysterium* from the world in which we live. In essence, it has de-sanctified the world, making it no more than matter to be exploited. Man and Nature become a mechanism, without spirit or soul.

In his book 'Origins of the Sacred – The Ecstasies of Love and War', Dudley Young considers how science has changed the way we see the world. He regards the change as beginning with the Renaissance and the start of a process whereby all that we once regarded as sacred was stripped of sanctity. Galileo was a significant

Towards a Philosophy of Shamanism

protagonist, who put the earth in orbit round the sun and knocked God – and man – off his pedestal. More recently, Charles Darwin placed man within the animal kingdom, not above it. In so doing, we lost sight of the hand of God and the soul of man. Darwin stripped everything of its soul, thus inverting the shamanic world-view, which placed animals alongside men as ensouled, sacred beings.

This has had a profound impact on the way we regard and treat the natural world, for, stripped of soul and sanctity, we may butcher the world at will.

Dudley Young uses Rembrandt's painting, the Anatomy Lesson, as a metaphor for the work of the scientist. He compares Rembrandt's dissected cadaver with Mantegna's painting of the dead Christ. The similarities between the two are striking. Mantegna's foreshortened image shows the dead Christ as supremely human and yet still divine. It takes a while to unpack what is happening in Rembrandt's near identical image. What seems, at first glance, to be a shadow on the lower half of the man's torso is in fact a gaping cavity from which the innards have been removed. It looks as if the corpse is having his hair combed by a barber. The 'barber' is, in fact, a barber surgeon, the comb a knife and the brains are being removed and placed in a 'dish' - the dead man's cranium. History has left us the name of the petty thief who is being dissected – Joris Fonteyn – and this adds to our sense of horror at the violation. The corpse is fresh-faced, young, dare I say beautiful. To it, we would ascribe the uniqueness and the sanctity of life. And yet it is being taken apart as if turning it into a bag full of blood and guts might disclose the great mystery of life itself. [3]

This is Science, disemboweling one of nature's masterworks in the pursuit of knowledge. Nature must be forced to yield her secrets. Whether that knowledge will be a benefit or a hazard is for history to decide.

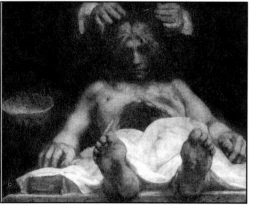

Rembrandt's Painting 'The Anatomy Lesson'

We have, as a species, benefited from medical research involving cadavers. That many of us are uncomfortable with such research is transparent. Even today, something of the sacred still clings to the human corpse. The outcry following the Alder Hey hospital scandal of the 1990s, where thousands of body parts from dead children were retained, indicates our disapproval of those who treat the human corpse as something less than sacred. Such attitudes are perceived as a hindrance to science, which simply sees a piece of human tissue in a jar of formaldehyde. Even to call it a 'heart' is dangerous, for the name implies love and life, pain and passion – things that are beyond the ken of science. The reckless desecration of thousands of graves by archaeologists the world over is also an indication of the spiritual and moral vacuum that science has created. It has taken the small

Towards a Philosophy of Shamanism

but insistent voice of the Native American, demanding the repatriation of the bones of their ancestral dead from the cardboard boxes of a thousand museums, to get some archaeologists to even recognize that there might be a moral issue involved in desecrating graves.

Scientists are not blind to the issues, but they are the high priests of our culture and the obscurity of their research papers means that the common man believes that science has the monopoly on truth. Science delivers - and the toys are there to prove it – like the toy we used to vaporize Hiroshima and Nagasaki and the countless souls those cities contained.

"Let's see a shaman do a trick like that," says the scientist.

We allow science the awesome authority to do as it wishes because we believe the pursuit of knowledge is good in itself. This belief is based on the confused idea that science alone delivers truth. All other world views – the religions, mythologies and philosophies of a thousand cultures are, at best, interesting fictions.

Young points out that Science is no different to Myth in its use of fiction. Science presents us with facts about the world. How we make sense of those facts – indeed, how some of them come to be disclosed in the first place – is a matter of fiction. The hypothesis, not the fact, is the foundation of all scientific knowledge and the hypothesis evolves, and may be finally abandoned.

Yet Science has provided where the shaman failed. Science is humankind's cornucopia – forcing even death into the shadows. The rich have abundant health, abundant food, and abundant years. Religion had its chance. Science delivered where Religion and Magic failed.

We must realize – and realize soon – that science without the sacred will fail us too, and far more catastrophically than its predecessors.

The price of unbridled technological advance is becoming apparent. The exploitation of Nature's resources and the elimination of the checks and balances She placed on human fecundity threaten the future of the planet. Few would dispute that our relationship with the planet is unhealthy - we can only describe our exploitation of nature as a kind of violation – a rape. Few would dispute that unless things change, the ability of the earth to sustain human growth and development will end in a matter of centuries.

The pursuit and exploitation of scientific knowledge is not, in itself, the problem. To argue that science is evil is clearly churlish. Rather, we need to recognize the existence of the sacred. Science needs the vision of the shaman. Science simply gives us facts. It does not tell us what to do with them. Young spells out the problem graphically:

Towards a Philosophy of Shamanism

> "Who was to say $E = MC^2$ would turn into an atomic bomb? Certainly not Einstein, the unfathering father, full of remorse. What makes this story monstrous is that it tells us where to find power, but is silent about when and where to use it. This silence, which claims to be high-minded, in fact allows unspeakable desires to slip from the shadows. Like a violent, psychotic child, this equation carries power without either self-control or the restraining hand of its father's law. Such power is intrinsically chaotic." [4]

Human life is sacred. The shaman knows that the anima, the soul, inhabits all things, making all things sacred. The animal also has a soul and is no less sacred. As shaman, I can see that soul just as clearly as a scientist sees the body. To abandon the sacred is to empty the world of meaning. It makes possible the monstrous. It is the story of Frankenstein who is destroyed by the monster he created. It engendered the mentality of the death camps of Nazi Germany and the appalling experiments carried out on human beings and animals in the name of science.

This is Science without the Shaman. We need to retrieve what primitive cultures still have and we have thrown away – the ability to see with our hearts as well as our eyes.

1.2. A Trip to the Movies
The Nature of Shamanic Ecstasy

> "There was a question I wanted to ask him. I knew he was going to evade it, so I waited for him to mention the subject; I waited all day. Finally, before I left that evening, I had to ask him, 'Did I really fly, Don Juan?'"
>
> *Carlos Castaneda*

The journey of the shaman is essentially a supernatural event. In his experience of flight, or in his dealings with the dead, the ordinary physical laws are suspended. At the same time his world is imaginary – that is, this suspension of the physical laws does not take place in actuality, but in the consciousness of the shaman. His experience is real for all that, for our very perception of reality is constructed in our imagination. Those who have witnessed or experienced true shamanic trance states cannot doubt the power and immediacy of the experience. At the same time, the shaman can distinguish between the physical world and the world of his visions. If he could not, he would be insane.

We have lost this ability to live and act in both the conscious and unconscious worlds. The shaman regards the phenomena he experiences in both worlds as authentic. The two worlds interpenetrate constantly and his precise role is to balance their impact on each other. To do this, both worlds must exist. A failure to regard both worlds as real leads to a failure of power:

Towards a Philosophy of Shamanism

"The effectiveness of a journey depends almost entirely on the shaman's absolute conviction that something substantial has actually been accomplished in these inner worlds. The sense of conviction or confidence is the shaman's greatest asset because by it he or she convinces others of its truth, and their joint belief creates a joint reality." [5]

Demythologizing – the stripping away of the meaning and value of myth in our lives - has cost us the shaman's inheritance. This shift in Western consciousness, which began with the Renaissance, can best be explained by a comparison with eastern culture, where, for many, the otherworld, with its gods and demons, remains substantial.

Indian Cinema dates back to the first days of the film industry and 'Bollywood' still makes more films for larger audiences than Hollywood. In the early days – way back in the 1920s and 30s, the cinema went to the rural millions of India on the back of a cart. When dusk fell the noisy machinery would whirl into action and the flickering images would materialize on the canvas screen. The most popular genre, in those days, were called 'Devotionals' – films about the Hindu gods – in which the costume and special effects departments stretched their skills to the limit to create an acceptable realism. The representations of the monkey god, Hanuman, picking up mountains or destroying a city with his burning tail, using puppets and table-top models, are still cited in Cinema text books as benchmarks in the development of special effects.

The relevant aspect of all this is the audience response. Offering worship – or puja - to the living manifestation of the gods as they appeared on the screen – was a not uncommon phenomenon. Unlike the painted statues of the temples, these images lived and moved, and inspired genuine awe. We may smile at the idea of the devout Hindu praying in front of a celluloid projection, but this devotion is no more or less absurd in a temple to a painted image of the god – or indeed to the star-filled heavens themselves.

The murti, or image of the god, is not the god himself nor is it worshipped as such. It is an image sanctified by the presence of the god, and acts as a channel for devotion. Through the eyes of the murti, the gods see me. My actions make the murti sacred, even divine. It personifies the Mysterium Tremendum, the awesome, uncontrollable forces of the great wheel of creation before which I am but a creature. The murti humanizes that which is beyond knowing and enables poor mortals to apprehend that which is beyond words and logic.

Joseph Campbell, when discussing sacred theatre, explains the status of the actor playing the god in the eyes of the primitive believer:

Shamanism and Sacred Landscapes

Towards a Philosophy of Shamanism

"The mask in a primitive festival is revered and experienced as a veritable apparition of the mythical being that it represents – even though everyone knows that a man made the mask and that a man is wearing it. The one wearing it, furthermore, is identified with the god during the time of the ritual of which the mask is a part. He does not merely represent the god; he is the god. The literal fact that the apparition is composed of A, a mask, B, its reference to a mythical being, and C, a man, is dismissed from the mind of the beholder." [6]

The universe has shrunk since those days, and Bollywood, as the Indian Cinema industry is fondly referred to, has a different message to sell. I see man – myself - and all my vanities on the cinema screen and I, not the gods, have become the measure of all things. Our imagination has shrunk and our ability to experience altered realities is damaged by the spiritual void created by the death of imagination. Our imagination stops at the screen, and the Cult of Celebrity has supplanted all other gods.

Something awful has happened. The window to the stars – my psychic sensitivities – my innate sense of the numinous, that sense of awe and dread by which I sensed the proximity of that *wholly other*, has been sledge-hammered by modern life and its environments into a kind of confusion. When I watch the sun set over the temple of Queen Hapshetsut and the cliffs that guard the Valley of the Kings, or experience the darkness and silence at the heart of the great Stone Age tomb of Newgrange, I am taken to that other place where the gods are present. But events have made me unthink this reality. I knew something was going wrong twenty-five years ago when I went to see a film called 'Close Encounters of the Third Kind'. When that vast spaceship with its awesome, cinema shaking sound effects finally appeared I felt the same awe as I did watching those sunsets at Luxor. I should have understood *that the gods were here too*– but I didn't. I felt tricked. Suddenly every temple and sacred stone, every church and tower, ritual and hymn seemed open to the charge of being manufactured by charlatans.

Consider this description of a Yakut Siberian shaman's words and actions, recorded by Wenceslas Sieroszewski in 1902.

> "The strong bull of the earth, the horse of the steppe,
> The strong bull has bellowed!
> The horse of the steppe has trembled!
> I am above you all, I am a man!
> I am the man who has all gifts!
> I am the man created by the Lord of Infinity!
> Come, then, O horse of the steppe, and teach!
> Appear, then, marvelous bull of the Universe, and answer!
> O Lord of Power, command!"

Towards a Philosophy of Shamanism

"When the spirit arrives the shaman begins leaping. He takes his place in the centre of the yurt and begins to drum and dance again. He flings himself into the air, he cries out wildly and he assumes the voice of the spirit... Now the shaman begins his ecstatic journey to escort the soul of a sacrificed animal to the sky. The shaman makes motions imitating a bird flying. Little by little he rises to the sky." [7]

I am distanced from Sieroszewski's experience by time and space. I am too late to witness the Yakut shaman as he danced and drummed and projected his frenzied energy at the Veil until it was sundered and he could begin his journey to the sky.

Sieroszewski was also too late. He watched the shaman with an anthropologist's dispassion as he danced from tree to tree, to which had been attached garlands of white horsehair and representations of birds. Time was, the Yakut people explained to Sieroszewski – not so long ago – when the shaman, dressed entirely in iron, would be seen to fly through the sky with his drum and the sacrificial animal. His power was such that it was his body, as well as his spirit that flew to the sky. Whether or not he physically flew may seem an odd question, but the very asking of it indicates that the Yakut tribesmen themselves no longer had eyes to see.

Already, the Landscape of the Soul is no longer visible to the devotees, who came to witness the shaman's flight. The shaman alone enters that different reality, and must paint for his people, in song, dance and careful recollection, his journey to the stars.

In his book 'The Teachings of Don Juan', Carlos Castaneda, a student of anthropology, became a disciple of Don Juan, a shaman of the Yacqui Indians, who uses hallucinogenic drugs to enter trance states. Don Juan provides few answers to Castaneda's insistent questions. Rather he guides Castaneda to the point where he can *experience* the answer for himself. Under the influence of datura, an hallucinogenic plant, Castaneda experienced flying. When he came back from a trance in which he flew as a crow, he asked Don Juan about the reality of his experience.

"There was a question I wanted to ask him. I knew he was going to evade it, so I waited for him to mention the subject; I waited all day. Finally, before I left that evening, I had to ask him, 'Did I really fly, Don Juan?'

'That is what you told me. Didn't you?'

'I know, Don Juan. I mean, did my body fly? Did I take off like a bird?

'The trouble with you is that you understand things in only one way. You don't think a man flies; and yet a brujo can move a thousand miles in one second to see what is going on." [8]

Shamanism and Sacred Landscapes

Towards a Philosophy of Shamanism

The question Castaneda asked his master is many-layered. How did Don Juan regard such experiences? In what sense can the experience of flying under the influence of an hallucinogenic drug be regarded as real?

It is the same question we may ask of the mystic, the dreamer, the shaman or the madman.

What is fascinating about the account of Carlos Castaneda's experiences is his naivete. He does not understand what is happening to him. His experiences do not cohere and he does not have the experiential framework of Don Juan to make sense of them. What we read might well be the experiences of someone who has taken LSD and had his visions guided by someone who talks him through the trip, as Don Juan does for Carlos.

So, what is the quality of the experience that the shaman achieves, however induced, and in what sense, if any, can it be described as real? How does it differ from simply going to the cinema and suspending my disbelief for two hours? If the film I'm watching can induce a state in which I think I'm flying, is this an authentic shamanic experience? In what way is the drug-fuelled trance of the techno-shaman of the dance floor different from that of the shaman of the rainforest? The shaman uses a hundred different methods to enter a trance or ecstatic state – hallucinogenic drugs, fasting, sensory deprivation, sensory overload with drumming and dancing, controlled breathing and so on. Isn't this just playing with the old neural synapses until they start firing in the wrong directions?

In his classic work 'The Varieties of Religious Experience', William James goes some way to providing a framework to understanding the ecstatic or mystical experience. He states that it has four distinct characteristics:

1: Ineffability. This means that the experience is such that it is impossible to put into words. The experience might almost be described as a state of feeling, rather than a state of intellect. Hence, the shamanic experience, like all other truly numinous experiences, is pre-rational. Words provide no more than a mythological framework, enabling the shaman to share the significance of his experiences – but not to share the experience itself. The words he uses are no more than signifiers. Don Juan argues that Carlos can only make sense of his experiences for himself. Such things cannot be taught.

2. Noetic Quality. Although they are experienced as emotions, the ecstatic or mystical experiences communicate truths or knowledge that cannot be understood in any other way. These experiences are deeply important – perhaps the most important a person can have. They are so important they can be life changing.

Towards a Philosophy of Shamanism

3. Transciency. Mystical experiences are often brief. Aspects of shamanic ritual are designed not only to induce the ecstatic state but also help sustain it. The interpretation of the experience afterwards, and locating it within the accepted mythology of the group helps to solidify an experience that would otherwise fade.

4. Passivity. James discusses the fact that many mystical experiences are facilitated by actions prior to the state coming into being. We might instance the use of hallucinogens or drumming and dancing to induce the trance state in which the ecstatic experience takes place. Once in that state, however – and this is what makes shamanizing dangerous in a culture unused to such things – the shaman is no longer in control of what happens. [9]

Many things can trigger these brief, ecstatic moments. Views (say from a mountain-top, after an arduous and dangerous ascent), a piece of music or finding oneself alone in an ancient tomb may all trigger an altered state of consciousness. These moments create a sense of *otherness*, a sense that there is vastly more to reality than appears on the surface. They might be dismissed as illusion but for that overwhelming sense of their significance. Certainly, someone who has never had such experiences will struggle to understand what I mean.

Rudolf Otto coined the word 'numinous' to describe that dimension of experience with which we experience the *wholly other*. He describes the experience as 'sui generis' – an experience that cannot be reduced to any other. To discuss it with someone else can only be done through the voice of personal experience – they must be brought to see what you see:

"There is only one way to help another to an understanding of it. He must be guided and led on by consideration and discussion of the matter through the ways of his own mind, until he reach the point at which 'the numinous' in him perforce begins to stir, to start into life and consciousness." [10]

It is the way of the shaman, who brings the novice to the experience first and searches for meaning afterwards. To those who have no such experience it will remain, literally, non-sense.

"Our X cannot, strictly speaking, be taught, it can only be evoked, awakened in the mind; as everything that comes 'of the spirit' must be awakened." [11]

Such experiences, whether induced or happening spontaneously, do not have much shape and clarity. One has experienced something more profound than the experiences of our daily lives – but when we come out of the trance or ecstasy, we are unable to give the experience sense or shape. In Carlos Castaneda's case, Don Juan talks him into a state of thinking that he is a crow and can fly like a crow. Without a rational framework to work with, we cannot articulate the non-linguis-

Towards a Philosophy of Shamanism

tic experiences of the unconscious. Invariably, we are drawn to the spiritual terminology of the culture of which we are a part to communicate the inexplicable. This should not alter the significance attached to such experiences by those who have them, provided the process of articulating those experiences does not end up with the telling of lies. It is vital that the reality and significance of the experience is not lost through the inadequacies of language.

The question that J.A.Symonds asks at the end of his account of experiences induced by anaesthetic drugs illustrates this point, and is reminiscent of Carlos Castaneda's question:

"Yet, this question remains, Is it possible that the inner sense of reality which succeeded, when my flesh was dead to impressions from without...was not delusion but an actual experience? Is it possible that I, in that moment, felt what some saints said they always felt, the undemonstrable but irrefragable certainty of God?" [12]

We are not talking about an intellectual argument for the existence of spirits and demons but about experiences that are more real than any other. That we have such experiences cannot be doubted. That such experiences are often profound and life changing is certain. When he returns from his 'flight' the shaman knows that he has returned to a different and indeed a lesser reality. The modern mind seems no longer capable of this dualism and prefers to test such experiences on the anvil of Science.

The charge of charlatanism can be leveled against a proportion of people who claim such experiences. Perversely, the more structured such experiences become in their content and in the way they are reported, the more likely it is that we are dealing with a degenerate account of a trance or ecstasy. Incoherence authenticates rather than falsifies our contact with the Unconscious.

St. John of the Cross, one of Christianity's great mystics, describes the ineffable or indescribable nature of his mystical experiences in his book, 'The Dark Night of the Soul':

" Fancy a man seeing a certain kind of thing for the first time in his life. He can understand it, use and enjoy it, but he cannot apply a name to it, nor communicate any idea of it, even though all the while it be a mere thing of sense. How much greater will be his powerlessness when it goes beyond the senses! This is the peculiarity of the divine language. The more infused, intimate, spiritual, and supersensible it is, the more does it exceed the senses, both inner and outer, and impose silence upon them.... The soul then feels as if placed in a vast and profound solitude, to which no created thing has access."[13]

Towards a Philosophy of Shamanism

Traditionally, the shaman serves his community and there is an expectation that he will 'report back' on his experiences in the Otherworld. The overwhelming evidence is that this otherwise indescribable experience is given form by the mythic backdrop of his culture. The same may be observed with Castaneda's training under Don Juan. His visions under the influence of the hallucinogens are initially interpreted for him – Don Juan's words transform Castaneda into a crow before he can experience flight.

Carl Jung argued that underlying such experiences and the mythological archetypes that are used to express them are constants that have their roots in what he called the 'collective unconscious'. These are the universal experiences of the unconscious that shape the mythologies of the world and the content of our dreams. Such archetypes Jung and others believed to be constant throughout human history - but the language used to describe them inevitably changes over time.

It is science and the conceptual frameworks of western philosophy that have taught us to regard religious experiences as false. Therein lies the contradiction of modern western concepts of reality. My experience was real – I experienced flight – and yet I am called to denounce the experience as false because it does not accord with that other reality of cold, scientific reason. Arrogant man, Nietzsche's Superman, must be the utter master of his world and the measure of everything. In such a world there is no place for that which may master him:

"Before God! But now this God has died! You Higher Men, this God was your greatest danger. Only since he has lain in the grave have you again been resurrected. Only now does the great noontide come, only now does the Higher Man become – lord and master...Very well! Come on, you Higher Men! Only now does the mountain of mankind's future labour. God has died: now we desire that the Superman shall live." [14]

In his 'Meditations', Rene Descartes asks if dreams are real. His answer is simple and provides the benchmark for all rational people. We question the validity of experiences if they are out of kilter with our normal everyday lives. If I wake up thinking I have just flown like a bird, I will say, 'well, I'm still in my bed; I obviously didn't fly anywhere.' The error of this type of reasoning is that I am using the same yardstick to judge all experience.

The point about Don Juan, is that his experiences under the influence of the hallucinogens do cohere as a separate and distinct kind of reality that reveals special truths. The same applies to the mystic and the prophet. To ask the mystic or the prophet if their experience of God is real, *when God is their supreme experiential reality*, is clearly nonsense. They *know* He is real. Whatever the techniques used by the shaman to achieve his or her experience the object is not to get out of their heads. It is to pursue a higher truth that only becomes transparent in that altered state – whether drug

Towards a Philosophy of Shamanism

induced or induced by drumming and dancing into a frenzy. Meditation can be used for a similar purpose. The Buddhist and the yogi believe that only through meditation can the apprehension of what is truly real be achieved. For the Buddhist, or indeed the Yogi, the world that we in the west have embraced is the world of illusion.

To believe in the spiritual realms without experiencing them is the demand made by the orthodox faiths of this world. To experience the spiritual realms and not believe in them is the demand made by science. The shaman's strength lies in the fact that he experiences the spiritual realms and that experience accords with the world-view of his culture.

Let us return to our cinema audience watching the 'Devotional' in that Hindu village of the 1920s. When a believer stands before the image of the god – be it movie depiction, masked actor or painted statue – he stands before the god. At one level, he understands that the representation is not the god itself. At a higher level, he experiences the existential reality of the god and objectifies that experience with the knowledge that the god also sees him. To challenge the reality of that experience is nonsense and demonstrates the same cultural blindness as Carlos Castaneda when he asked:

"But did I really fly?"

Yes, our dreams dissolve with the dawn and the spirits conjured by the shaman vanish with the opening of our eyes. The shaman flew, to be sure, but no one saw him move. The reality of his experience, like all experiences, is measured by his own perception of them. Yet Science has nothing stronger to offer. We are the product and the prisoners of our own experiences. This is the only reality we know and to reject it is a counsel of despair, for we allow others to call us liars on a daily basis. All experience, dreams, waking thoughts, the scientific experiment, the mathematical calculation – or flying through the star-lit sky to the throne of God Himself - are part of our unified and seamless interaction with all that is. To the end of my days my eyes alone are the guarantee of what is real. The rest is hearsay.

> "Our revels now are ended… These our actors,
> As I foretold you, were all spirits, and
> Are melted into air, into thin air,
> And like the baseless fabric of this vision,
> The cloud-capped towers, the gorgeous palaces,
> The solemn temples, the great globe itself,
> Yea all which it inherit, shall dissolve,
> And, like this insubstantial pageant faded,
> Leave not a wrack behind…."
>
> *The Tempest*

Towards a Philosophy of Shamanism

1.3. Earth and Humanity
The Function of Myth in Shamanic Experiences

> "We have no symbolic vocabulary, no grounded mythological tradition to make our experiences comprehensible to us."
>
> *Stephen Larsen*

In his book, 'Shamanism and the Mystery Lines' [15], Paul Devereux discusses the underlying shapelessness of the ecstatic experiences of the shaman. Form, he says, is given to the shamanic experiences by the mythological backdrop onto which the shaman paints them. This concept explains why the Christian who has a 'near death' experience, thinks he sees Jesus at the end of the tunnel of light, whereas Hindus will 'image' Krishna. It has been argued that these inconsistencies undermine the validity of such experiences. They do nothing of the kind. We use the language of our culture to describe all our experiences. Thus, one person describes the bright figure as Jesus, another Krishna, and a third the Buddha. It is the inadequacy of language, not the inauthenticity of the experience, which creates the variety of responses to what is seen. The shamanic experience is ineffable – beyond words - in character. Communication of such experiences requires a common language, and the mythology of the community with whom the shaman shares his experiences provides that common language.

Let me explain with reference to the passage from Shakespeare's 'The Tempest', which I quoted at the end of the last chapter.

To celebrate the betrothal of his daughter Miranda, Prospero, once Duke of Milan and a magician, uses his magic art to create a masque in which the goddesses of ancient Rome – Ceres, Juno and Iris appear. This celebration of seasons, of the harvest and fecundity is followed by a dance of reapers and nymphs. It is as if, for a few brief moments, the entire pantheon of the classical world lives once more under Tuscan skies. These gods were themselves once elemental spirits – of the orchard, the fields and hearth, worshipped by other names long before the wolf suckled Romulus and Remus and Rome itself was born.

The gods and spirits of a thousand generations are, as in the pageant of Prospero, sustained by our imaginations. They live in the teachings of our priests, oracles and seers, in sacred scripture and songs, in the dreams of witches, druids and shamans. They live in our heads and are fed and nourished there. To name them is to give them life; to build a temple to them is to free them to walk amongst men. Such is the power of myth. To the educated audience of Shakespeare's day, classical literature had awakened the

Towards a Philosophy of Shamanism

Renaissance and re-populated Olympus with the gods of old. What else could Shakespeare do but explain his vision to his audience in language that made sense to them? It is the same for the shaman.

Joseph Campbell, J.G. Frazer and Carl Jung all suggest that the many gods of the Greek, Egyptian, Indian and Norse pantheons may be transposed back into a few powerful archetypes that have their origins in a forgotten ancestry that goes back to the Paleolithic and beyond. The stories of the gods are patterned to reflect our most primordial of human desires, fears, longings, and aspirations. They reflect our frail and all too brief existence, set against the cosmic drama that is forever unleashed around us. Myth reflects the reality of the Unconscious. The language of myth attempts to break down the barriers of words and concepts that separate us from the experience itself. It is, like the language of music, able to touch the emotions in an elemental way, and communicate directly with our hearts.

Myth is now taught to our children as story. Aspects of it are translated into films, fantasy novels and computer games. At the academic level, we talk about *demythologizing*. In the Christian tradition demythologizing begins in earnest with the 'Liberal Quest for the Historical Jesus', led by such scholars as Schliermacher in the nineteenth century and Paul Tillich in the twentieth. If we strip Christ of the potent archetypal image of the Dying and Resurrecting God, who is Oak and Holly King and the harvest wheat, who is Osiris and Mithras whose flesh gives life - what are we left with? He becomes – merely – a nice man with a moral message, who died a violent death.

Demythologizing is the process of stripping away the mythic content from sacred texts in order to reveal the kernel of historical truth – if it exists. It seeks to remove the supernal and the superstitious in order to isolate the 'fact' behind the fable.

In the aftermath of Charles Darwin's 'Origin of the Species', British scholars of the late nineteenth century regarded myth as only of value in what it revealed about the primitive or 'savage' imagination. It was in this climate that J.G.Frazer wrote 'The Golden Bough'. In his biography of Frazer, Robert Ackerman refers to a contemporary of Frazer, Edward Burnett Tylor, an influential scholar of the period. Tylor wrote in 1881:

" Myth is not to be looked on as mere error and folly, but as an interesting product of the human mind. It is sham history, the fictitious narratives of events that never happened. It is both reasonable and useful, however, to inspect myths and other religious statements and extract from them whatever factual content they may have, discarding the quantities of rubbish that remain." [16]

Towards a Philosophy of Shamanism

Ackerman describes the 1880s as an era in which the growth in knowledge about religious beliefs and practices from around the world, including shamanism, was used to assert the superiority of the rational, scientific mind. It was the age of cultural, as well as political imperialism. For some, the mythologies of primitive cultures prefigured the 'superior' religion of civilized men – Christianity. Others argued - Frazer amongst them – that the intellectual bankruptcy of all religious beliefs and practices is made transparent by demonstrating the primitive and superstitious antecedents of all religions.

The enthusiastic rejection of the role that myth plays in our lives was founded on the idea that man, now that he has 'come of age', no longer needs myth. The transparent superiority of the rational mind was there for all to witness. It took the bloodbaths of two world wars to shake the intellectual complacency of those who regarded scientific rationalism as in every way superior to the products of religion and superstition.

In rejecting the old myths we are likely to create new and far more dangerous myths. Paul Tillich described our fundamental need for "an object of ultimate concern." If the old God is dead, humans will make another. Nazi Germany is a prime example of a society founded on a new mythology, born of the conscious, profane mind that has rejected the soul and the supernal.

We need myths. Myth is the road to the Otherworld and without myth we are forced to live in the shadowland of cold objectivity.

Myths reveal the how and why of human existence. They tell of the cost of human arrogance, as in the tale of Prometheus who is chained to a rock and tortured for stealing fire from the gods. The story of Pandora reveals the price that must be paid for the unlimited exercise of human curiosity. Both stories speak profoundly to the nuclear physicist and the genetic engineer. Myth gives drama, meaning, and morality to human actions because they reveal, underneath whatever masks we choose to wear, the truth of our human character. Myth enables the unconscious self to speak in the conscious world and thus prevent psychosis. For Carl Jung, this was the essence of psychological wellbeing.

The decline of myth has had other serious consequences for the intellectual and emotional well being of our culture. Some have fled the harsh, two-dimensional world of scientific materialism and taken refuge in religious fundamentalism. The latter part of the twentieth century saw a resurgence in fundamentalism within all the major religious traditions. Fundamentalism is dangerous because we allow others to tell us what to believe. The unquestioning belief in another man's vision saw a number of instances of mass suicide in obedience to a cult leader. Shamanism is anathema to the funda-

Towards a Philosophy of Shamanism

mentalist, for each trance or ecstasy brings visions that challenge the tenets of orthodoxy. Fundamentalism is based on the unquestioning acceptance of the word of another. Shamanism is based on what the individual has experienced for themselves to be true.

Having experienced the emptiness of a godless universe, some now turn to exotic cultures to create a 'pick-n-mix' mythology to fulfill their spiritual needs. Paganism, for many, is not about a rediscovery of old roots but a borrowing of new and shallow stock from around the globe. Shamanism will wither on such a vine. If that self-same mythological backdrop is simply 'borrowed' then it serves to invalidate rather than reinforce the ecstatic vision. The use of cultural borrowings opens the practice of shamanism in modern western culture to the charge of charlatanism. The western shaman must practice his art – physically and psychically – in his own back yard.

The shaman cannot do his work without experiencing the truth of his myth. To validate myth we must draw on our own experiences of the conscious and unconscious worlds. We must root our mythology in our own earth and in our own sacred spaces. The importance of basing mythogenesis on our personal relationship with the land becomes apparent when we realize that this relationship is the root of all myth. The myth of the dying and resurrecting Christ, just like the dismemberment and reintegration of Osiris, celebrates the fecund earth that yields new and joyful life. The miracle of spring is something that we must witness for ourselves and intuit in all its profound joy if the old gods are truly to live in our hearts once more. We must experience to the core our status as creatures of the earth, formed from a tiny seed by sun and rain and the goodness left in the earth by the endless cycle of growth and decay. It is a truth beyond all doubting that the earth is the womb of all life, including our own. Our unconscious self knows this with the kind of truth that is not fractured by the inadequacy of words. Our unconscious self is the earth in that it is the sentient manifestation of life untrammeled by the arrogance of words. Our unconscious self knows the dynamism of the spirit - the anima - that moves all things.

This sense of oneness with the earth and the spirit of the land cannot be an intellectual construct or a cultural borrowing. It must become our own most profound relationship. This relationship with the earth and those who move and sleep in her is the root of the shaman's power.

The shaman is the original mythmaker. He is the dancer who affirms the truth that all of Nature's children have a soul. He affirms that man has responsibilities with regard to his Mother that he ignores at his peril. The shaman can heal – but his power to heal is limited by the faith of the community in what he has seen. Unless we share his myth, he can do nothing.

PART 2
Shamanism and Sacred Landscapes

2.1. The Spiritual Orphan
The Significance of Landscape in Shamanic Culture

ALTERED STATES OF CONSCIOUSNESS, however achieved, cannot deliver the true shamanic experience. The shaman already sees the spirit world he is about to enter, for it connects seamlessly with the landscapes of ordinary life. The spirit world is everywhere. Every sickness and unusual occurrence can be laid at the door of spirits and demons. All life is a manifestation of *pneuma* – the spirit that gives life.

Shamanising requires that we connect with the spirits, or anima in all things. We must feel their overwhelming presence. For the shaman of old this was easier. The bones of the ancestors were –literally - all around him. He could communicate with animal souls as well as those of humans. The spirits came close in the night. In his world, the living, the dead, and the land are one. He walks the ancestral paths and becomes a conduit for the power in the earth.

For the shaman the land is spiritualised. The land is a living, sacred entity that tells the story of all the worlds.

What does the land mean to you and me?

I have moved house several times during the course of my life. The paths that I walk and the places that are special to me have changed too. The urban landscape was the backdrop for all my childhood memories. I grew up in the shadow of crumbling Victorian cotton mills. Trees and grass existed only as open spaces between oppressive urban sprawl. When things changed, it got worse, for the high rise blocks of my teen years took away the sky too. I was disconnected from the land and spiritually homeless, adrift in a world where an affinity to place was rare. I didn't belong anywhere.

The urban environment disenfranchises us from the land, as do the office blocks, factories, motorways and shopping malls in which the majority of us now live and earn a crust. We have stumbled on this new way of living almost by accident and in a matter of as many generations as you can count on two hands. We have not yet, and may never adjust to the fractured spiritual horizons this has engendered. In his great work 'The Phenomenon of Man', Teillhard de Chardin summarizes the predicament of modern man:

"Advanced as it was in many ways two centuries ago, our civilization was still based fundamentally on the soil.... The type of 'real' property, the nucleus of

Shamanism and Sacred Landscapes

the family, the prototype of the state, (and even the universe) was still, as it is in the earliest days of society, the arable field.... Then, little by little, as a result of the 'dynamisation' of money, property has evaporated into something fluid and impersonal, so mobile that already the wealth of nations themselves has nothing in common with their frontiers.... What is troubling us intellectually, politically and even spiritually is something quite simple. With his customary acute intuition, Henri Breuil said to me one day: 'We have only just cast off the last moorings which held us to the Neolithic age.'" [1]

As a spiritual orphan, I am careless of place. The land may feed me but I owe it nothing. I can buy and sell it like any other consumer trash. It is no longer my Mother, but real estate of a certain value.

When the Native American or the Aborigine talk of land, they do not think of a block or parcel of land contained by boundaries and owned by right of a piece of paper. How can you own that of which you are a part? It is like saying my hand owns my body. It *is* theirs, rather, by virtue of the footprint of their ancestors along the hunting paths and their ancient camping grounds by the streams and waterholes. It is theirs by virtue of the bones of the dead and the sacred objects that had been returned to the earth in the high places, where the Great Spirit is close. Place is defined by rivers and rocks, mountains and forest, camping ground, dancing ground and the bones of the dead. To die is not to be lost – it is to return to the very earth from which you are formed and to lie with the great ancestral dead with whom you are and always will be one.

I know that I do not have to be still to have this affinity with place. The wandering clans of our Palaeolithic ancestors may well have ranged over considerable distances, as do the Australian Aborigines, the Yakut of the Siberian Steppes and the nomads of the Sahara to this day. But the paths and stopping places are constants, they walk in the footsteps of their ancestors, though they now cross the borders of several countries and may have citizenship of one or none. Indeed, it is in the very essence of movement, of re-claiming our relationship with the land by walking in it, that we build our relationship with it. Gypsies and travellers know this.

What matters to native people is the path. What matters is to walk. In order to reconnect with the shaman I must reconnect with the land. The land embodies that other self that I have lost. It is the key to the Unconscious – to the land of the spirits and the ancestors. The shaman walked the same paths I now follow to the mountains and the sea. He named these paths. He named the rivers and brooks, the rocks and the caves. He built the tombs of his ancestors where they might be seen from afar and set up standing stones to guide his way.

Shamanism and Sacred Landscapes

The search for the shaman's path involves both an inner and outer journey, reflecting the fractured worlds of our conscious and unconscious lives. The evidence of his life is out there in the landscape. All human activity transforms the land, even if it is only in terms of associated memories, place names and ancient standing stones. These activities have left traces that can be read and understood.

Ritual landscapes are, essentially, shamanic. They are a concrete expression of the belief that we can move from one reality to another. The design of ritual landscapes and sacred spaces facilitates that altered state of awareness in which the gods become close. A stone circle or a megalithic burial monument is a *liminal* space. By liminal, I mean a barrier or point where one kind of reality meets another. They are meeting points for the sacred and the profane, for the living and the dead, for gods and men. They create a focus for the community where they may communicate with the spirit world through prayer and sacrifice. For the shaman, the ritual landscape is where the barrier dividing the sacred and the profane can be readily breached. They are places where, to use Dion Fortune's phrase, "the Veil is thin."

Just as a laser focuses and channels the energy of light, the earthen long barrow or the passage grave channel and utilize the energy of the ancestral dead. They are a focus for the pneuma, the breath of the world, and are often found in spaces already made sacred by anomalies in the landscape or the activities of the ancestors.

We no longer understand such landscapes. We use the tools of the scientist to search for the power in the stone and turn the megalith builders into mathematicians, astronomers, and engineers. They were all of these things and none. Mathematics, astronomy, and engineering were not an identity for the megalith builder, but tools. The people who designed the stone circle and the long barrow were technicians of the sacred and they created their monuments and the rituals held within them to utilize the power of the pneuma.

We no longer have faith in the realms of the spirit and thus the shaman is stripped of power. The meaning is not only stripped from our heads, it is also stripped from the land. We leave the land naked, ready for exploitation by the person who only sees an opportunity for profit. It becomes empty space, not place.

The shaman cannot dance in a barren landscape.

Our relationship with the land is crucial to our well being. Landscapes are sedimented with the human experiences of countless generations. They reflect the inner landscape – that of the unconscious, which is also sedimented with the experiences of countless generations. The two landscapes act as mirrors. Sacred landscapes are physical manifestations of the collective unconscious.

The shaman's technique has, as its theoretical and practical bedrock, a methodology of renewing our relationship with pneuma by moving through a landscape in which pneuma is manifest and remythologises our experience of it.

The message of the book is that we can rediscover those landscapes, which will give us a home and our soul's repair. We must learn to read the landscape once more in order to awaken the soul within.

2.2. Remythologising the Earth
Understanding the importance of Place.

> " The Aboriginal landscape is one replete with a highly elaborate totemic geography linking together place and people. Formed in the Dreamtime, the landscape provides an ancestral map for human activity…. The grounding basis of Aboriginal mythology and enduring proof of its correctness was the evidence of design in the world in the sense of pattern, shape, form and structure, which was itself proof of intent." [2]

The Aboriginal Dreamtime is written in the landscape. It is stronger than that – the Dreamtime *is* the landscape and to walk the paths of the ancestors is to give the ancestors life. In urban cultures, where we have become separated from the land, we have had to find other ways of preserving our sacred heritage. The priest becomes the repository of myths, temples confine the deity, and duly sanctioned prophets are the only channel to the Divine. There is no place for the shaman once you have priesthood. The land becomes desanctified and the process of alienation begins.

Urban life brings with it an obsession with time. Our ancestors were keen to note the passing seasons accurately – but for them time was circular – and the concept of 'progress' largely meaningless. The Egyptians, with their six thousand-year-old civilization, sought to preserve a wisdom that had its roots in a time beyond remembering. Our linear sense of time and our desire for progress lets the past fall away as *history*, a mere, written remnant. Time renders our ancestors insignificant, and their bones and possessions survive as museum curiosities. They are dead things, neutralized even to dust by the passing years.

With hunter-gatherer communities, the past is alive. Time is "collapsed into space", with the names and adventures of the ancestors and the spirits reactivated every time a path is walked. The ancestors move in a timeless world, where their

Shamanism and Sacred Landscapes

journeys are mapped along familiar paths and watercourses. A year, a thousand years, ten thousand years are all the same. The ancestors still sleep where they fell.

I have experienced 'the collapse of time' on many occasions. Indeed, I believe it impossible to shamanize unless you can be with the spirits of those whose physical lives are over. In the same way, space is collapsed so that my spirit may become one with that of a bird who flies high above. To be one with a bird or the spirit of the dead is not a matter of summoning spirits. This is the work of the necromancer, not the shaman. It is a matter of experiencing the collapse of time and space so that you and the spirit share the same experiential space. One such personal experience will serve to illustrate the point.

In the summer of 1997, I was privileged to assist John Gowlett, of Liverpool University, on his dig at Beeches Pit, a Lower Palaeolithic site some 350,000 years old, near West Stow, in Suffolk. Here, by a river that had flowed a third of a million years ago, archaic humans camped. The task I was engaged in was to free a two ton block of clay which contained the remains of a hearth, by whose warmth our ancestors had made their flint tools, butchered their prey and slept those countless years ago. The block was to be crated, craned out of the pit and taken by road to Liverpool University. As a mature and eager student, I often continued work when my youthful companions had left for their evening meal and the pub. On the night before the block was due to be removed, I worked late at the pit, finishing the cradle of timber and scaffolding in which the block was to be lifted. Several bolts could only be accessed by way of a deep, narrow trench that we had dug behind the block. I was, literally, in the earth, as I struggled to tighten the scaffolding clamps beneath the block.

I had spent the day placing into little plastic bags and labelling the fragments of their lives – burnt flakes, chipped from a flint core and the tooth of a horse. I was handling their possessions, living in their space, and breathing the very molecules of their lives from so very long ago.

Suddenly, they were there. I sensed them not with my eyes or ears but with a sense that rose up my spine and froze my blood. I heard them and saw them and though I lay as still as I could, I know they saw me. That one inflexible dimension, time, had shifted, so that I shared that same night fire with those who made it. The fire burned again, I heard the knapping of the flints and their chatter as they cut up the kill. They welcomed me and through me, however briefly, they lived again and gave me their power.

It was a profound experience in which, what Rudolf Otto called the *Mysterium Tremendum*, overwhelmed the senses and became, not a 'still, small voice', but a supreme reality. The illusion of time, of my individuality, had fled, and my fellowship with those men and women was complete.

Shamanism and Sacred Landscapes

When the experience ended – was it no more that a few seconds? – I was left with a deep sense of pain that we were destroying a place imbued with a kind of sanctity. I was the last who would be able to lie in the darkness by this ancient hearth - ever. Those archaic men and women who had danced their magic by this fire would be gone with the dawn, their energy dissipated to the four winds. The very earth where we had sat together was being ripped apart, and like so many sacred treasures, was destined for the clinical environs of an anonymous university laboratory. It is a metaphor for our treatment of the entire planet.

I am sure that many of you can identify with such experiences. And for every person who has witnessed such things there is a different explanation as to their meaning and value. For all, surely, it is at least about a profound sense of place - that the presence of earth and water, of animal and ancestral spirits make a place sacred, not just for me, but for all who use the eye of the soul. Such places become a focus or 'centre', to use Eliade's word, for the rituals of the shaman.

Thus, the same spot that was once a camping ground for our Mesolithic ancestors becomes an earthen long barrow in the late Mesolithic. This in turn becomes a megalithic tomb in the Neolithic and a stone circle in the Bronze Age. The Celt builds his fort here or buries his dead. The Christian attempts to control the 'spirit of place', with a church and a graveyard. The bones of four hundred generations mingle in the dust.

The Australian Aborigine understands all this. Each clan carefully preserves the memory of the paths, camps, dancing grounds and burial places all the way back to the Dreamtime. But this is not an historical act – it expresses the felt and experienced presence of the ancestral spirits as a constant, sharing the same landscape of the soul:

"The landscape was one in which the ancestors hunted and gathered, and so every aspect of it has generalized ancestral connotations. It contains the bodies of the ancestors inside it and is also the metamorphosed forms of the ancestors, the tracks they made and the imprints of their bodies.... A large number of these ancestors turned into stone at their final resting point. The Rainbow Serpent, one of the most potent of the ancestors in western Arnhem Land, swallowed other ancestors and then was forced to vomit their bones, forming rocky sandstone and quartzite escarpments. Quarrying stone for axes, is, therefore, quarrying the bones of the ancestors. The axes are themselves formed from ancestral bones – hence their potency." [3]

Ayers Rock is perhaps the most famous example of such sedimentation of memory. There is virtually no place on the surface of the rock that is not

Shamanism and Sacred Landscapes

a named ancestral locality. It encodes the mythologies of many tribal groups, crystallizing a world-view, as it has done in the same way for countless generations.

Anthropologists refer to this phenomenon as animism. It is regarded as something that pertains to primitive peoples, who regard everything as having a spirit of a life and these spirits being interconnected, one with the other and with all physical things. The concept breeds a reverence for all of nature, for all that is nature has a soul and lives.

The earth and its living soul is the source of the shaman's power, not the hallucinogenic drug that lifts the veil of words and enables him to see things as they really are. It is the dancing ground, not the drug, which facilitates the visions of other worlds.

This leaves the twenty-first century shaman with a problem. To what do I connect when I seek those new realities? Where do I go to tap that sedimentation of spirit ancestors with whom I connected as an initiate? If I have no dancing ground I have no power. My spiritual journey is a fiction and the work of a charlatan.

We must not be drawn into the temptation of believing that we can adopt a shamanic culture from anywhere. Other peoples see the world differently and in copying their ways we risk making a mockery of their culture. These profound differences of culture were highlighted by Carl Jung in his 'Alchemical Studies'.

"Western imitation is a tragic misunderstanding of the psychology of the East, every bit as sterile as the modern escapade to New Mexico, the blissful South Sea islands, and central Africa, where 'the primitive life' is played at in deadly earnest while Western man secretly evades his menacing duties…. Our task is to build up our Western civilization, which sickens with a thousand ills. This has to be done on the spot, and by the European just as he is, with all his Western ordinariness, his marriage problems, his neuroses, his social and political delusions, and his whole philosophical disorientation." [4]

The shaman initiate must begin his quest for power in a new relationship with earth and landscape. It is in the essence and individuality of the shaman that he must find his own. But how does the spiritual orphan, who is long since separated from his ancestor spirits and the paths they walked find that special place? The writing of Carlos Castaneda gives us our first clue.

2.3. Sacred Landscapes
The Problem of Relationships and Identity

The first lesson that Don Juan teaches Carlos Castaneda is that some places are safe and some places are dangerous. When a shaman leaves his body to accomplish his tasks, he becomes vulnerable. His soul and body are separated and a malign spirit may steal body or soul. One night, when they are sat on the veranda of his hut, Don Juan's tells Castaneda to find the 'spot' where he feels most comfortable. This 'spot', Don Juan explains, is where Castaneda will feel happy and strong.

"Several times I asked for a clue, or at least a hint, as to how to proceed in locating a point where I felt happy and strong. I insisted and argued that I had no idea what he really meant because I could not conceive the problem. He suggested I walk around the porch until I found the spot." [5]

Castaneda does not know where to begin. He tries every method he can think of but cannot find the spot in which he feels happiest. He has no rationale to identify such a place. He does not know how he should feel even if he finds it. Crawling, rolling around the floor, systematically sitting in every spot fails to locate that special place.

In time, by trial and error, Carlos identifies two spots. In the first spot, he feels sick and afraid. In the second spot, he simply falls asleep. It is the spot where he instinctively feels safe and can let go. He does not know how he identified the two places. It might be argued that he used something that is innate in us, some primordial instinct, through which we sense – unconsciously – the places where spiritual forces may harm us and where we are safe. It is the sense we should use in choosing a place to live if we want happiness to be the criteria of a wise decision.

This sense cannot be taught. It is something that we know intuitively – by using our instincts. It is not something new. As a species, we had this ability before we learned to walk upright four million years ago.

Modern 'alternative' spirituality has tended to localize spiritual 'hot spots'. Glastonbury, where I have chosen to live, is one such place. The unseen 'energies' that seem to be at play here are experienced by many. But these places are not good for everyone – far from it – and those seeking strength from place must learn to trust their instincts. There is a tendency to focus on a narrow range of such ancient monuments that have become places of pilgrimage. Stonehenge and Avebury are examples of ancient sites that have become a focus for individuals and groups seeking the power of place.

Shamanism and Sacred Landscapes

For some, such places will become their spiritual home. For others, the experience can be psychically damaging. For all of us, it is foolish to let others choose where our own 'special spot' is. This is something that we can only do for ourselves. In describing five sacred paths later in the book, I seek only to provide the training that will enable you to identify the power – both benign and malevolent – for yourself. We no longer have the sedimentation of ancestral bones and experiences to help locate our special 'spots'. If the location of such 'spots' is important as a spiritual anchor, where do we begin to look? Where do we begin the search for the benign dust of our shaman ancestors?

Nature herself begins the process, isolating rocks and streams, mountains, and lakes as wind, rain, ice and the very heaving of the earth sculpt the landscape. She creates spaces that express her dynamic and become repositories of her creative power.

Humans also vest power in the landscape when we name these spaces. Once they are named they become *places* and we can share their identity with others. In his book 'A Phenomenology of Landscape', Christopher Tilley describes the process:

" The naming and identification of particular topological features, such as sand dunes, bays and inlets, mountain peaks etc., settlements and sites is crucial for the establishment and maintenance of their identity. Through an act of naming and through the development of human and mythological associations such places become invested with meaning and significance.... The bestowing of names creates shared existential space out of a blank environment." [6]

A first point of reference in reawakening our sense of place can be to explore those places that were invested with meaning by our hunter-gatherer ancestors and re-invested with meaning by the generations that followed. We may use such places to explore both our conscious responses and to stimulate the promptings of the unconscious.

The Hill of Tara in County Meath, Eire, is an outstanding example of sedimented meaning that has produced responses from countless generations and against which we may measure our own responses. The oldest monument on the hill of Tara, the Mound of the Hostages, dates back to 3500BC. Since that time, the hill became the site of a Bronze Age rath, or fortified house, and several Celtic forts and monuments were erected here. The hill became the crowning place and the seat of the High Kings of Eire and it is said that over forty of Ireland's kings ruled from Tara. A thousand years after the crowning of the last of Tara's kings, rebels made a stand for National Independence on Tara and are buried where they fell. It was from Tara that Daniel O'Connell denounced the Act of Union in 1843 and began the long fight that was to lead to Irish Independence. It is a place suffused with the

Shamanism and Sacred Landscapes

myths of countless generations. It is sacred ground, which embodies the history, culture, and ethnicity of a people in its sculpted slopes.

The power in these fields is palpable. The sanctity of the earth is enriched with the great events that took place here from the mythical events associated with the Mound of the Hostages and the Fort of the Kings, to the burial of martyrs in the fight for Irish liberty in modern times. Irish myth brings its heroes and heroines to Tara to act out the great events of the collective imagination of a people. Long before the high kings ruled from Tara, it was the home of the gods. At Tara the Tuatha De Danann - the goddess Danu and her divine family –dwelt until they were displaced to the faerie hills in the Time of Men. The Tuatha De Danann have their origins in the great spirits that symbolise the beneficial aspects of nature – light, life, fertility, wisdom and good. [7]

The spirits have been slow to leave Tara. Even as late as the beginning of last century, the society of British Israelites, convinced of the supreme sanctity of Tara, tore apart the Rath of the Synods searching for the Ark of the Covenant.

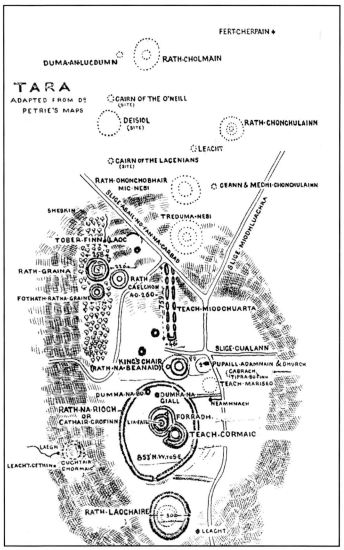

Map of Tara – after Flinders Petrie

To the cold rationality of capitalist ethics and scientific endeavour, there is nothing here. These are agricultural fields with a certain commercial value for farming and a potential for tourism. To the people of the Irish Republic, it is a vastly important part of their national consciousness. It is, in every sense of the world, sacred ground and the embodiment of the Irish spirit.

Our paths through the landscape, our naming of the landscape to create sacred spaces, the building of monuments and the rituals we enact therein, become, therefore, a personal history, a social identity and a quest for meaning of both individuals and a people. They make shamanism possible because sacred landscape provides the shaman with the language for sharing his experience of the spirit world.

'Special Spots' may confront us suddenly and catch us unawares. We may visit a place for the first time and sense an affinity and the special energies that a particular locale has to offer. It may be that our relationship with place will grow over time as we sediment more experiences and memories in a particular locale. We will grow in knowledge of a place and develop a strong sense of its history.

Our relationship with landscape in a modern capitalist society is not always as connected as it is at Tara. Ancient monuments can become a commodity like any other and are marketed as such. Monuments may achieve 'celebrity' status and suffer accordingly. Thus, I must endure my visit to Newgrange with crowds numbered in their thousands – to experience what is substantially a reconstruction where ancient stones hide the reinforced concrete structures that make it safe for the tourist. Hype determines meaning and the media creates new myths for our ancient monuments, which obscure the subtle truths that we can only experience through our own senses.

Christopher Tilley aptly describes the mentality that is tearing the heart out of our landscapes and monuments and turning them into a commodity:

"...Landscapes, buildings, places and localities in contemporary society seem to have lost, or be in the process of losing, their value and significance. The space created by market forces must, above all, be a useful and a rational space. Once stripped of sedimented human meanings...the landscape becomes a surface or volume like any other, open for exploitation and everywhere homogeneous in its potential exchange value for any particular project. It becomes desantified, set apart from people, myth and history, something to be controlled and used." [8]

The sanctity of place is not intrinsic to any landscape – not even the venerable stones of Stonehenge. Sanctity is invested in a landscape, both in the present and through time. It lies precisely in the emotional and psychic relationship between an individual and place, or groups of people - however that group is defined - and place. The investment of sanctity represents the soul of a people. It determines our attitude to place. It needs to be seen as the most significant dimension of sacred place, for without it, the Stones are nothing. The Power lies in the relationship of subject and object but it is no less real for that. Myth encodes such relationships in a timeless language that speaks directly to the Unconscious, allowing people across the generations to share a unity of response to sacred place. Those who despoil ancient monuments in order to

Shamanism and Sacred Landscapes

maximise value-for-money or scientific knowledge, would do well to remember this.

When such a relationship no longer exists our treatment of sacred place can become problematic. I have already referred to the 'marketing' of Newgrange. What happened to 'Seahenge', however, demonstrates our cultural inability to deal with sacred landscapes when we don't know how to 'market' them.

Seahenge prior to its removal

©Norfolk Museums
& Archaeology Service.
Photo by Mark Brennand
& Jason Dawson.

The discovery of 'Seahenge' happened during the Autumn of 1998. This astonishing monument, exposed by the action of the sea off the coast of Norfolk, England, revealed a virtually intact wooden circular structure with an upturned tree bole at its centre. This discovery, dated by dendrochronology to 2050BC, presented an almost unique insight into prehistoric religious practices. [9]

In its original state, it had consisted of a great, central upturned oak bole, surrounded by a stout palisade of 55 split oak branches, which were so close together that it would have been impossible to see inside the sacred circle. Access to the interior was by a cleft in one of the branches, which was blocked by another piece of timber. Its similarity to monuments built for shamanic rites is startling.

Shamanic rituals of ascent into the sky are often symbolized by the ascent of a tree. The Cosmic Tree, or the Axis of the World is conceived as occupying the centre of the world. By climbing it, the shaman undertakes "an ecstatic journey to the centre." (Eliade P120-123) Descriptions of such trees set up by the shaman sometimes feature a palisade around them. It is perfectly valid speculation to suggest that the upturned tree bole and its attendant palisade were for shamanic purposes, perhaps providing a means, in this instance, to descend into the Underworld.

The sea and the erosion of the peat lens in which Seahenge had been preserved threatened the site. It was also situated in an S.S.S.I. – a site of Special Scientific Interest run for English Nature by the Norfolk Wildlife Trust. Because of the sensitive nature of the site, visitors were discouraged and information about the find restricted. Media interest changed all that and there were unseemly arguments between Druids, Archaeologists, local people, the Norfolk Wildlife Trust and other 'interested' parties over the future and ownership of the monument.

Shamanism and Sacred Landscapes

Seahenge – The removal of the central bole.

©Norfolk Museums
& Archaeology Service.
Photo by Mark Brennand
& Jason Dawson.

The press and TV carried images of various 'Druids' and other groups of 'pagans' performing a plethora of rituals amidst the rotting remains of Seahenge. One suspected that the presence of the cameras, rather than spiritual compulsion, was the primary motive for their bizarre rituals. The various interest groups fought for control of this sacred space – and destroyed it. This incident, perhaps more than any other in recent times, expresses our inability to understand what sacred space means. Our ancient monuments have survived the depredations of millennia because past generations respected them and felt the presence of the sacred – benign or otherwise – in these locales.

The decision to remove Seahenge to 'safeguard' it from the erosive effects of the sea was made hurriedly and without any serious thought as to what would be done with the structure once it was removed. One outcome discussed was that they would be simply buried deep in the sand as the cheapest method of 'preserving' it. There are now plans to reconstruct Seahenge at Flag Fen, a major Bronze Age archaeological centre of research and Visitor Centre in Norfolk. Relocation of the monument is better than burial – it remains, however, a commodification of sanctity and a typical solution of a society where all outcomes must be seen to be 'cost-effective'. [10]

A sacred landscape was destroyed precisely because no one had ownership in any spiritual sense. English Heritage has learned its lesson and a second 'Seahenge' that has emerged from the sand nearby will be allowed to die a natural death - barely noticed, now the media circus has departed. [11]

The contrast between the treatment of Tara – where excavation is now all but banned – and Seahenge, highlights our problem with sacred places. Native Americans and Aborigines have fought for, and substantially won the right to prevent further desecration of what remains of their sacred places. The thirst for 'scientific' knowledge and the desire to commodify and present such places to an ill-informed and 'profane' audience was rapidly destroying a cultural heritage that had endured precisely because it was once understood. Underneath the destruction of the monuments is the destruction of the land itself and our relationship with it. Shamanism cannot work where there is such disharmony between people and the land. Whatever form the practice of shamanism takes in our own society, its essential role must be to re-define and rescue that relationship.

Shamanism and Sacred Landscapes

2.4 Exploring Inner Landscapes
Carl Jung and the Psychology of Shamanism

> "If you spend the night on Arthur's Seat, on the summit of Cader Idris, and survive to tell the tale, you will descend the mountain a poet or a madman."
>
> *Old Welsh saying.*

There are a number of techniques available to the shaman to attain the altered state of consciousness that Eliade termed 'ecstasy'. Some are dependent on the use of hallucinogenic drugs. Eliade himself regarded the use of drugs as a degenerate practice. Shamans also use the body's natural physiology to attain ecstasy. These experiences are by no means confined to the shaman. The shaman interprets his ecstatic state in a particular way. Other physical events and accidents may trigger the so-called 'shamanic flight'.

People who have 'near death' experiences describe journeys that resemble those of the shaman. With the rapid responses of paramedics in the more affluent cities of the world, there are literally thousands of people who have been 'brought back from the dead'. In reality, these people have not died. They have experienced oxygen starvation with the stopping of the heart and the flood of endorphins produced by the heart attack and other shocks to the system. People typically describe travelling through a tunnel of light, meeting 'ancestors' and heavenly beings, and being able to look down on their own bodies.

Military airforce pilots, training in giant centrifuges which test their responses to large 'g' forces, record similar experiences. Pilots are positioned so that blood pools downwards, thus depriving parts of their brain of oxygen. Some pilots describe euphoric experiences similar to the 'near death' experience of heart-attack victims. We may thus begin to understand how the dancing, drumming, whirling and hyperventilation created by shamanic performance generates altered states of consciousness. The whirling of the whirling dervish will also redistribute blood in the brain and can create a similar sense of altered consciousness or 'ecstasy'.

Physical exhaustion, solitude and sensory deprivation may also trigger states of altered consciousness. Sensory deprivation works by removing the usual over-burden of stimuli that batter our senses in normal life. In dark, silent environments, deprived of human company our senses become enhanced and more highly attuned. Feeling *our flesh creep* and *our hair stand on end*, are classic physiological responses to darkness, silence and

Shamanism and Sacred Landscapes

that feeling of being utterly alone. Tiredness adds to the likelihood that ecstasy will be achieved as dream states merge with conscious experiences. There are dangers with this technique. Panic can set in easily when we are alone and every sense is straining into the void. This is why knowing your environment and *feeling safe* in it are very important. In time, alone in the darkness of a windswept moor or the enclosing silence of an ancient tomb, *you will see things*. The courage of the shaman lies in confronting the outpourings of the unconscious and drawing knowledge and power from the beings encountered, whether they come as guides or adversaries.

Does understanding the 'mechanics' of ecstasy devalue the experiences they generate? Understanding how to stimulate different experiences does not render them false. We all know that for all the pleasures and pains we experience, there are corresponding physiological phenomena. Understanding how my body creates the feelings of love does not mean that I am not in love. Taken to its extreme, we would end up denying the reality of all experiences unless they are observable by others, ideally in laboratory conditions. This confuses both the work of science and the nature of human experience. The great Copernican coup – that the earth spins on its axis and the sun does not 'rise' or 'set' at all, began a trend whereby 'scientific method' dictates how the world 'ought' to be seen in a scientific age. The reality of human *experience* is that the sun rises and sets. The reality of *my experience* is that the spirits I encounter in a trance state exist. I take what other people tell me about the world on trust. My world is the world that I see.

A shaman must regard his experiences as the first point of reference and his grip on life. True, he must learn to differentiate between the products of the physical world, and the products of the imagination. But one is no less real than the other, and both interact to disclose the fullness of our universe and the richness of the human psyche.

Successful shamanizing requires a conceptual or experiential framework that renders otherwise inchoate experiences meaningful and valid. This is where our relationship with particular landscapes is important. The ecstasy takes place in, and is enacted through physical landscapes that are shared with others. The power of landscape to provide an interpretive language is enhanced both by the presence of ancient monuments and by a belief that ancestral shamans also drew power from these locales. The experience of moving through a landscape and building a mythology of action and experience within it provides the experiential framework through which the shaman communicates what he sees to others. Most importantly, movement becomes a kind of search for access to the otherworld. The shaman may search through physical movement or *journey in the imagination* through those self-same landscapes.

Shamanism and Sacred Landscapes

Shamanism and Jungian Psychology

"Apparently we have not always been human beings. We are beasts of this earth who have undergone a most peculiar event, a change into something rich and strange. It must have first happened somewhere, sometime, to someone. We are a transformed animal, a creature with culture. We may think we are normal, but we are not. We are changelings."

Rogan Taylor.[12]

The book of Genesis describes how the first man and woman were tempted by the Serpent to defy God and eat of the Tree of Knowledge of Good and Evil. This defiance of our 'original' nature made us unique amongst the animals. We became moral beings, capable of introspection, and aware of our mortality. Filling our belly and fornicating was no longer enough. A different hunger created the psychic urge to build pyramids and split the atom. But we remain, fundamentally, a beast, and the priest must wipe his arse with the same hand that holds the Body of Christ.

The journey we have undertaken, from beast of the trees and the savannah, to painter, musician, architect, astronaut and nuclear warrior, was made possible by our imagination. Even as primitive hunter-gatherers, we peopled the landscape with spirits and demons. As simple nomad our imaginations pierced the heavens and tore down the veil that hid the throne of God. We *imagined* the universe long before we built telescopes to observe with our beast's eyes what we had always dreamt of. It is with our imagination that we may journey both outwards and inwards, into the past and the future, to draw together the strands of what we are and what we could become. Adam and Eve *imagined* themselves as gods, and by defying their nature as beasts, they began mankind's journey to the stars.

The spiritual power we once had has been crippled by our positivist attitudes. We now associate the idea of something 'imagined' with something 'false'. 'You imagined it' means 'it didn't really happen'. Our ancestors didn't think that way. They regarded all experiences as real. Some experiences belonged to this world and some were otherworldly. For our ancestors, *journeys of the imagination* were just as real as physical journeys.

The shaman's technique is to use his imagination to journey inward and outward by projecting his *inner world* on to the world *out there*. To do this successfully he must regard the inner and outer worlds as distinct but real. He frees his imagination to wander using shamanic drumming, trance dancing and hallucinogenic drugs. Arctic shamans and Native Americans use extremes of solitude and physical hardship to achieve the same end.

Shamanism and Sacred Landscapes

Freeing the imagination from the constraints of our conscious, rational selves lies at the heart of the technique. Affirming the reality of our ecstatic experiences is what imbues them with power.

Carl Jung achieved the same end using what he called *active imagination*. The technique requires that the person is *their own shaman*, creating their own spiritual landscapes as a way to knowledge and self-healing. The reason for the emphasis on self-healing is explained by Marie-Louise von Franz, a life-long student of Carl Jung, in her book 'C.G.Jung – His Myth in Our Time':

"Active imagination is done by the analysant alone. No image, no reaction to the inner images is prescribed for him: it is the lonely way to one's self, unprotected, but also undisturbed by any guiding hand. The role of the guide, which is preferred by some therapists who use other techniques, is dangerous to the therapist himself. It can seduce him into the "pride of the shaman," of which much that is evil is reported in primitive myths. In addition it robs the patient of the thing he needs the most, which is free inner responsibility." [13]

The purpose of *active imagination* is to access the world of the unconscious in a way that enables us to objectify and thus engage with the products of the unconscious. To do this we have to suspend the rational faculties that repress the unconscious. We then have to find new techniques for engaging with the strange creatures and experiences that emerge. Marie-Louise von Franz outlined the methodology used by Jung:

"In principle active imagination consists in suspending the critical faculty and allowing emotions, affects, fantasies, obsessive thoughts or even waking dream images to come up from the unconscious and in confronting them as if they were objectively present.... An alert, wakeful confrontation with the contents of the unconscious is the very essence of active imagination.... Fantasies can be objectified by writing them, by drawing, painting or by dancing them. A written dialogue is the most differentiated form and usually leads to the best results." [14]

The original shamans objectified their 'fantasies' by describing them to their audiences. They became a medium through which an entire community might experience the power of the spirit world. This power is absent where there is no belief. The spirit world must be experienced as real. At the same time, it must be objectified by manifesting the experience in some way in the world *out there*. The traditional shaman narrates his story through dance, song, speech, the plastic arts and by figurative and abstract drawing. The technique suggested by Jung is that of the old, as

well as the new shaman. But the narrative must be regarded as the record of a real event, not of fiction.

I have had interesting conversations with people who have experienced shamanic journeying and share their experiences through dance or drawing. My own personal technique is to come to terms with my experiences through writing. Initially I found it difficult as a technique because writing inevitably involves the *corrective* processes of the rational self engaging with the products of the unconscious. Instead of regarding this as *fictionalising* experiences, I now think of the process of committing such experiences to paper as a dialogue between the conscious and unconscious self through *active imagination*. It is, inevitably, creative. Anyone who understands how the shaman works will understand that the interpretation the unconscious experience requires a creative template. It is the integrity of the experience and its affirmation as real that validates it.

"Whoever does this will begin to understand that *every fantasy is a genuine psychic process or experience which happens to him*, and he thus becomes the active and suffering protagonist in an inner drama. But if he merely looks at the inner images, then nothing happens. One has to enter into the process with one's own personal reactions. There are those who do this in fact but with a fictitious personality, that is, the reactions are not genuine reactions but are "acted," while somewhere in the background there is the thought that this is all "just fantasy"; then, too, nothing happens and inner development comes to a standstill." [15]

We all know that young children have vivid imaginations and often lead potent psychic lives. Left to their own devices, they will populate the world with the products of their imagination. Growing up can often be a process of closing the doors to the child's psychic worlds and forcing them to live with the harsh realities of two-dimensional adult life. Jung argues that we have to learn to repair the damage we have done to our imaginations. We allow our conscious selves to interfere with the products of the unconscious to the point where spontaneous fantasies are suppressed completely or reduced to the status of daydreams. We need to develop the ability to liberate the psyche and thus live fully in both our conscious and unconscious lives. [16]

Some modern western shamans make use of active imagination and these practices have drawn significantly on Jung's work. One such shaman is Professor Michael Harner, who invites us to think differently about how we regard the products of the imagination. He has this to say on the subject of the imagination:

Shamanism and Sacred Landscapes

"Imagination is a modern Western concept that is outside the realm of shamanism. The word 'imagination' already prejudges what is happening. I don't think it is imagination as we ordinarily understand it. I think we are entering something which, surprisingly, is universal – regardless of culture. For the shaman, what one sees – that's *real*.... If you can't trust what you see yourself, then what can you trust?" Michael Harner. [17]

Harner, a practicing shaman, argues that we must learn to trust our experiences once more. We must learn to trust ourselves. In so doing we become a master of our world, with power over our inner and outer lives. We learn to visualize and manifest the forces ranged against us and thus to control them. It is precisely the technique that Carl Jung developed using his 'active imagination' technique.

Carl Jung described his own experiments with the unconscious as life-changing. The forces that he drew from those inner realms not only existed within his imagination, but became externalised. The trick lay, as it does with the shaman, in learning to control the forces released from the unconscious. Jung refers to these projections from the unconscious as 'fantasies'. He used the word 'fantasy' to distinguish these experiences from the everyday world, rather than to challenge their authenticity. As with the shaman, he recognized the different realities of the conscious and unconscious worlds.

Jung gave the personalities that emerged from his unconscious an external persona in order to give them an identity independent from his own. He then interacted with them as creatures independent of himself. One such 'personality' was Philemon, who first appeared to him in a dream:

" There was a blue sky, like the sea, covered not by clouds but by flat clods of earth. It looked as if the clouds were breaking apart and the blue water of the sea was becoming visible between them. But the water was the blue sky. Suddenly there appeared from the right a winged being sailing across the sky. I saw it was an old man with the horns of a bull. He held a bunch of four keys, one of which he clutched as if he were about to open a lock. He had the wings of a kingfisher with its characteristic colours.... Philemon and other figures of my fantasies brought home to me the crucial insight that there are things in the psyche which I do not produce, but which produce themselves and have their own life." [18]

"In my fantasies," says Jung, "I held conversations with him, and he said things which I had not consciously thought.... He said I treated thoughts as if I generated them myself, but in his view thoughts were like animals in the forest, or people in a room, you would not think that you had made those people, or that you were responsible for them.... It was he who taught me psychic objectivity, the reality of the psyche.... At times he seemed to me quite real, as if he were a living personality." [19]

The important factor about these 'fantasies' is that Jung distinguishes between the product of his own mind and that *other self*, the unconscious. He had conversations with Philemon. He described Philemon as representing a force that was not himself. He was, to Jung, what a spirit helper might be to a shaman. Philemon became his guru, his teacher, just as shamans are 'taught' by the spirits of ancestral shamans.

Jung was moving onto dangerous ground – and he knew this – and it was necessary to develop a strategy to avoid the dangers that these relationships posed. The shaman faces the same dangers. Jung developed a method for controlling the figures projected from his unconscious. By personifying the products of the unconscious, one becomes distanced from them. By bringing them into a relationship with conscious thoughts, they remain real but less powerful. They remain autonomous, and that can be uncomfortable, but we know where we stand in relation to them and thus the dangers of psychosis can be avoided. [20]

Jung was, in effect, advocating the shamanic principle of being clear about what belongs to the conscious *middle* world and what belongs to the otherworld and comes from *above* and *below*. A shaman is not a schizophrenic. He is strong in his own identity and is in control of the products of his imagining.

Controlling the spirits is vital. The essential difference between mediumship and shamanism is one of control. The medium allows himself or herself to be *taken over* by the spirit who uses the body of the medium to communicate to the living. The practice involves a temporary loss of soul. The shaman seeks to *control* the spirit as best he can – by making offerings, cajoling, and sometimes by outright confrontation. In his actions within the world of his visions, the forces that threaten to overwhelm him are translated into the figures of the collective mythology of his people. Thus they can be understood, contained, and made to respond in ways that repair the psychic damage that is being experienced by the individual or group he is seeking to heal or protect. It is for this reason that shamanizing outside of a defined conceptual framework is dangerous. To contain and direct the powers that the shaman raises, he must provide the masks that the characters in the psychic drama wear.

The need for caution remains. When we create, through our imagination, a thing that seemingly exists independently of our *conscious* self, it may become just that – *independent*. Only by consistently containing these manifestations by giving them a voice in his writing, was Jung able to keep them under control.

Shamanism and Sacred Landscapes

Shamanism and Sacred Landscapes

Some of Jung's experiences serve as a warning of what can go wrong. The energies that he was drawing from his unconscious were beginning to externalise themselves to the point of affecting his family. It seemed to him that he was unleashing psychic forces into his very household that needed to express themselves:

"It began with a restlessness, but I did not know what it meant or what 'they' wanted of me. There was an ominous atmosphere all around me. I had the strange feeling that the air was filled with ghostly entities. Then it was as if my house began to be haunted. My eldest daughter saw a white figure passing through the room. My second daughter, independently of her elder sister, related that twice in the night her blanket had been snatched away; and that same night my eldest son had an anxiety dream.... The atmosphere was thick, believe me! Then I knew that something had to happen. The whole house was filled as if there were a crowd present, crammed full of spirits." [21]

Jung was beginning to realize that his experiments had become a real danger. He needed to give the products of his unconscious a voice before they consumed him. The shaman, too, must give voice to the spirits or risk destruction. The outcome of this overwhelming sense of possession was the writing of 'The Seven Sermons of the Dead'. The book was written during the course of three evenings. Once he had started to write the ghostly presence evaporated. [22]

Jung tried to make sense of the experience, which he described as 'parapsychological phenomena' in which the *numen* of the archetype had been projected abroad. Of even greater interest to the student of shamanism are the experiences that led up to this crisis. A fantasy that Jung had prior to these paranormal disturbances was completely shamanic in nature:

"Shortly before this experience I had written down a fantasy of my soul having flown away from me. This was a significant event: the soul, the anima, establishes the relationship to the unconscious. In a certain sense this is also a relationship to the collectivity of the dead; for the unconscious corresponds to the mythic land of the dead, the land of the ancestors. If, therefore, one has a fantasy of the soul vanishing, this means that it has withdrawn into the unconscious or into the land of the dead. There it produces a mysterious animation and gives visible form to the ancestral traces, the collective contents. Like a medium, it gives the dead a chance to manifest themselves. Therefore, soon after the disappearance of my soul the "dead" appeared to me. This is an example of what is called "loss of soul" – a phenomenon encountered quite frequently among primitives. [23]

Shamanism and Sacred Landscapes

This passage is highly significant for understanding shamanism. Jung's power came after he had experienced a loss of soul, which then journeyed into 'the land of the ancestors'. This single experience was enough to generate shamanic power because the door to the spirit world, once opened, stays open.

There are lessons to be learnt from this for the modern shaman. If shamanizing is to be *real* and not merely a game, the risks must be recognized. Some have argued that many shamans are schizophrenic and the risks of schizophrenia, or at least paranoia, are very real. Strength of mind is required, as well as the will and the means to share the experiences with others. That they are set down on paper or opened to rational discourse in some other way is vital. That way, the shamanic experiences may sit alongside our conscious experience and the relationship between the two mediated. This is done through a personal or a shared mythogenesis. That mythogenesis, created and shared by the shaman with his community or another individual through 'acting out' or storytelling provides the foundation that creates the shaman's power and safeguards him from psychological harm.

The sharing of a 'transpersonal' vision that speaks to our common humanity, and can be identified with the archetypes of the Collective Unconscious is what makes shamanism possible. Madmen have nothing to share – their 'visions' are often self-obsessed and bound up with their sickness. The shaman uses what Larsen describes as a 'consensual reality', where a community shares the experience of the shaman as *real* to all. In painting his experience to his audience, the shaman projects his experience as myth. The myth *is* real, but projecting it as myth means that he and his audience distinguish it from the everyday world. This separation from ordinary reality makes it more, rather than less potent because it renders it *super-natural* rather than merely *natural*. [24]

Active Imagination and the Use of Landscapes

"True wisdom is only to be found far away from people, out in the great solitude, and it is not found in play but only through suffering. Solitude and suffering open the human mind, and therefore a shaman must seek his wisdom there." Igjugarjuk, Caribou shaman of the Canadian Arctic.

The use of lonely and isolated physical landscapes both to engender ecstasy and as a means of portraying the psychic landscape to his audience is common amongst shamans. Alongside the Jungian technique of active imagination it can provide a robust and meaningful technology for shamanic journeying. Instead of subduing the conscious self through the

Towards a Philosophy of Shamanism

use of hallucinogens, this technique requires a committed affirmation of the reality of the products of the unconscious. This affirmation is aided by using landscape to construct a relationship between the conscious and unconscious worlds.

Much modern shamanic practice is a group or social phenomenon. Would-be shamans 'shamanize' with like-minded people. There is nothing particularly peverse in this – the shamans of Siberia and South America usually 'perform' before an audience.

The shaman does not, however, find his power in the public performance. He must leave his community behind and find power in the quiet places. When he goes, he goes alone. The template for these journeys often lies in a past solitude as dark and as deep as the grave. Without that prior experience, the initiatory 'hell' of psychic destruction and reconstitution in the great and lonely wastes of this world, he can have no power. Great suffering comes first. The power to become a shaman is obtained in isolation and that power is sustained through isolation. The same principle applies to every visionary since the times of Abraham, Jesus and Muhammad. It is when we are alone, in the deserts, on the mountain-tops and wandering the icy wastes of this world that the spirits speak to us.

I would like to quote from Igjugarjuk, a Caribou shaman, made famous through the writings of Rasmussen, the Danish explorer. The Caribou were a nomadic people, living in the arctic wastes of the northern extremities of Hudson's Bay. Igjugarjuk attained his shamanic powers through his experiences of starvation and extremes of cold. He sought his earliest encounters with the spirit world in the harshest of solitudes and became a shaman only when his self-imposed hardships had brought him close to death. Once he became a practicing shaman he avoided any kind of showmanship. When called to heal it was in solitude that he sought his strength.

"When I had quite become myself again, I understood that I had become the shaman of my village, and it did happen that my neighbours or people from a long distance away called me to heal a sick person.... When this happened the people of the village were called together and I told them what I had been asked to do. Then I left the tent or snow house and went out into solitude, away from the dwellings of man.... If anything difficult had to be found out, my solitude had to extend over three days and two nights, or three nights and two days. In all that time I had to wander about without rest, and only sit down once in a while on a stone or a snowdrift. When I had been out long and had become tired, I could

Towards a Philosophy of Shamanism

almost doze and dream what I had come to find out.... These days of 'seeking for knowledge' are very tiring, for one must walk all the time, no matter what the weather is like and only rest in short snatches. I am usually quite done up, tired, not only in body but in head, when I have found what I sought." [25]

Eliade also reports the use of isolation as the essential dimension in the self-initiation of shamans. The elder shaman teaches the initiate to isolate himself in a lonely place – beside an old grave or a lake to await the experience of death and dismemberment followed by resurrection. [26]

We can understand how Igjugarjuk's 'technique' worked. The extreme isolation of the arctic wastes and the lack of contact with others made his senses much more attuned to the voices of the otherworld. He often walked until he was exhausted. In this state, where it is difficult to stay awake, hallucinatory experiences often follow. The unconscious world comes into the fore in a way that makes interaction with the conscious self possible. For those seeking a comfortable shamanism, the message is stark – the real shaman suffers for his art – and it is at the extremes of what humans can endure that we find the gateway to the shaman's power.

Landscapes can thus be used both to stimulate shamanic vision and to create a psychic anchor by connecting those experiences with real locales. The raw products of the unconscious, though real enough, lack definition. They are a pre-rational phenomenon, originating from a time before words, and are therefore beyond the direct comprehension of the conscious mind. They belong to the Jungian collective unconscious. The products of the unconscious have to be 'brought down' and framed by images and experiences that are meaningful to the conscious self. Using active imagination to engage in mythogenesis within a known physical landscape creates a framework that enables the shaman to maintain, in their own understanding, the difference between their conscious and unconscious worlds and to communicate that understanding to others.

Shamanism and Sacred Landscapes

Shamanism and Sacred Landscapes

Part 3.
Interpreting Shamanic Landscapes

Preface
Reading the Monuments

"As soon as a man comes to life, he is at once old enough to die."
Martin Heidegger

THE HYPOTHESIS explored in the following chapters is that: many of the landscapes of ancient Britain were monumentalized by our Neolithic forbears to honour their ancestors and to facilitate the public performance of shamans in doing business with the dead. The hypothesis is rooted in the fact that the most commonplace monuments in the ritual landscape of the Neolithic are those that celebrate the dead. The great earthen long barrows, passage graves, cursus monuments, rock carvings and stone circles that grace our Neolithic landscapes all served a recognizable purpose – that of creating ritual spaces to communicate with those who inhabit the realms above and below the middle world of men.

In communities where belief in spirits is important, ordinary folk practice their faith in those places where the spirits are known to reside, and it is communities, not individual shamans, who express this common experience in the creation of monuments. Often, a natural feature, such as an unusual rock formation, a spring, a hill, or even a forest clearing might engender the experience of a place as 'sacred'. Likewise, evidence of ancestral activity, such as ancient pathways, burial grounds, or even occupation sites with the remains of flint knapping from long ago, might prompt the creation of monuments by later generations. Many locales were probably already embedded in the mythology of the people, long before they were monumentalized with big stones. They are shamanic landscapes because they express the beliefs of a community for whom the presence in the land of powerful spirits of the ancestral dead is an existential reality. Stephen Bergh, an archaeologist researching the Neolithic tombs of the Cuil Irra in Sligo, Ireland, explains the function of monumentalizing the dead:

"Making the dead visible through the monuments in the landscape, is a way of giving them a material identity in the present and future society. The ancestors become thereby possible to manipulate and by this a pressure instrument within groups striving to achieve, keep or enhance a certain position." [1]

The shaman has his part to play as mediator between the living and the all-powerful dead. As Eliade himself comments in his review of shamanic cosmology, shamanism shows the closest dependence on funerary beliefs, concerning itself, as it does, with the movement of souls of the dead from one world to the next.

Interpreting Shamanic Landscapes

To understand the central role of the ancestors in Neolithic society and, indeed, in many surviving cultures, we need to rethink our understanding of time. We in the West have inherited a biblical concept of time, which is essentially linear. The world has a beginning and an end and the past is experienced as 'history'. We measure time in years and the greater the number of years between our time and the time before the more distant and remote it seems. Primitive cultures take their cue from nature and have a circular concept of time where souls and the natural world are part of an endless cycle. The communal burials of the Neolithic in Britain indicate that in our relationship with the ancestors time is irrelevant. They remain eternally present and their power does not fade. They are part of the past and the future. We can know the shamans of the past because they renew themselves with each generation. The nexus is the landscape, where memory abides in rocks and streams and in the great monuments the ancestors raised to fix the meaning of one time for all time.

Monuments serve to change or attenuate the meaning of natural landscapes. The construction of a sacred monument is an act of imagination that expresses a preconceived reality. By trying to understand these 'signed' landscapes we can begin to reconstruct some of the experiences of those who built them. In turn, we can reconstruct the inner landscape in which the altered realities that engendered these monuments can be made present to our own imagining. The shamans have left these signs to guide our way, which we may learn to recognize and read.

Passage grave, Loughcrew, County Meath, Ireland

Interpreting Shamanic Landscapes

3.1. Shamanic Maps.

"Every landscape has its own spiritual meaning."
Piers Vitebsky

The power of the shaman comes from bringing the landscapes of the unconscious to bear on the landscapes of our daily lives. This means travelling to the *otherworld*, where the spirit of all things is visible to those who have the ability to shamanize. At the same time, the spirit world is projected *out there*, and is found in the woods and streams, in quiet valleys and on mountain-tops. It is the reconciliation of flesh and spirit.

Landscapes are the theatres of human activity. Unlike other animals, human beings construct reality, both in the way we choose to perceive things and in the way we create settings in which to act out the dramas of life. The shaman is the actor par excellence, who manipulates reality both for himself and for his community. He transforms the landscape by constructing symbolic artifacts, such as the Cosmic Tree, and by investing the landscape with a mythological content. Movement through the spirit world is explained with reference to physical movement through a shared topography. The shamans of aboriginal communities around the world use their familiar landscapes to share their visions with the community they serve. Piers Vitebsy cites the example of the Sora shamans of Orissa, in northeast India:

"The Sora mental map is the same as that of the physical landscape over which groups of people walk, work and dispute every day of their lives.... Dialogues with the dead bring together a crowd of people who all agree which spirits are where and who has been absorbed into each of them.... All members of the society share the same cosmos and landscape. In a shamanic culture, mapping one's mental state on to a geography of somewhere outside oneself is not just the privilege of the shaman, but is a basic way of talking about one's emotions and social relationships. This may be the geography of the universe, or it may be a geography of the trees and bus-stops outside someone's house" [2]

In time, and over generations, the landscape becomes sedimented with the shaman's mythogenic projections. In some instances, this mental mapping will remain as an imaginative construct. In other instances, simple depositions may take place in the form of food offerings or simple wooden spirit dolls. Or, the sedimentation of myth in our sacred landscapes may be expressed by building monuments, which make hidden truths available to the believer in the form of icons of stone and wood. The mythic landscape may also be expressed in the form of tales and folklore that become attached to particular locales and in place names. Certain locales may become so special that they are used as repos-

Interpreting Shamanic Landscapes

itories for the ancestor's mortal remains. We become embedded within a landscape, literally, through the roots of our ancestral bones.

A ritual landscape is much more than a repository of memory. The monuments that humans add to the landscape are themselves a manifestation of belief and our emotional response to the transcendent. Our experience of the Divine is crystallized in sacred architecture. Such structures may be 'read back', perhaps not with the precision of language, but certainly in a way that taps the same emotional wellspring that inspired the builders. The function of cursus monuments, such as the Stonehenge cursus, serves to connect monuments and provide a flow of experiences. They would have been redolent with meaning, most of which we can only guess at. Only our unconscious world and those same, rooted emotional responses that provide an unbroken link with our shaman ancestors can enable us to share in those rituals and experience the shaman's dance in the dust of the millennia. The monuments are an expression of belief, and, at the same time, an encapsulation of a spiritual response to the world. To return to Rudolf Otto's terminology, the circles of wood and stone express our apprehension of the 'numinous':

"One can hardly escape the idea that this feeling for expression must have begun to awaken far back in the remote Stone Age. The motive underlying the erection of those gigantic blocks of stone, as at Stonehenge, may well have been originally to localize and preserve and, as it were, to store up the numen in solid presence by magic." [3]

Monuments were built to speak to us, just as much as they were erected to speak to the people who built them and their immediate descendants. Those who build in stone do so to speak to all generations to come.

At the same time, monuments are designed to provide a theatre for specific rituals. The builder already knows the rituals that will take place in them and in that sense, these monuments map the movements and experiences of the participants. Rituals use a specialized language of words and movements – they follow a set pattern. The realities that such rituals depict belong to the eternal and remain unchanged through time. Rituals embody the transcendent and are the means by which suffering humanity enters into communion with the Divine. Shamanism undoubtedly has its part to play in shaping our understanding of the transcendent and hence in shaping the rituals of our earliest societies. If we read the monuments correctly we may indeed gain access to the mindscapes of our own ancestral dead. As Richard Bradley stated in his Rhind Lectures:

"In ritual the past reaches right into the present and the two cannot be separated." [4]

Interpreting Shamanic Landscapes

Our oldest surviving monuments date back to the close of the Mesolithic period and the beginning of the Neolithic. In Britain, the Mesolithic spans the time between the retreat of the last Ice Age, twelve thousand years ago, and the arrival of settled farming communities in the early Neolithic, six thousand years later. The arrival of agriculture and the development of new technologies, such as the polishing of stone axes and the manufacture of pottery define the Neolithic. The arrival of agriculture and pastoralism would not have been a sudden transition and we can assume that the lifestyle of the hunter-gatherer and his shamanic practices continued throughout the Neolithic and into the Early Bronze Age, when sedentary lifestyles became more common.

3.2. Shamanism and British Prehistory – The Mesolithic Age

The great shamans of the Northern Hemisphere are still to be found in those landscapes that overpower human sensibilities – the arctic wastelands and the endless expanses of tundra that border the coldest regions on earth. Here life remains an elemental struggle, with brief summers and winters of endless night, driving snow and merciless winds that carry death in their teeth. The Siberian tundra of today is Britain 14,000 years ago, when the ice sheets that covered most of Wales and northern Britain had begun their retreat north. As the ice retreated, hunters migrated from southern Britain and across the land bridge from Europe in pursuit of the herds of deer, horse and elk that possessed the new land. Before these post-glacial migrations of the Mesolithic, tiny Upper Paleolithic communities had eked out a living on the edges of the ice sheets, burying their dead in the caves of the Cheddar Gorge and Paviland Cave in Pembroke, where the skeleton of the famous 'Red Lady' was found. We must remember that these 'cavemen' were not naked savages, but cultured men and women who wore fine sewn garments of softened hide, and their counterparts in France created some of the greatest art the world has seen on the walls of their caves. A fragment of bone, found in Pin Hole Cave, Creswell, Derbyshire, and dating back to 12,000 BC, has a line carving that appears to depict a deer-headed 'dancing sorcerer', linking these communities with the practice of shamanism. [5]

The 'Sorcerer' of Les Trois Freres (after Abbe Breuil)

The people of the Mesolithic lived in small communities, perhaps forty strong, surviving through seasonal migrations that maximized the opportunities of the harvests of the forest and sea. Their relationship with the natural environment was intimate, their knowledge of the pathless wastes as instinctual as that of

Interpreting Shamanic Landscapes

Carved bone from Creswell Crags, Derbyshire, showing dancing 'shaman'

migrating birds. As the world grew warmer, hazel and pine trees of the post-glacial period gave way to forests of oak, hazel and pine. These forests abounded with game, the rivers teemed with fish and the human population of Britain began to expand from a few hundreds to thousands.

As with all hunter-gatherer communities their world was driven by the invisible powers of the spirit world. The forces that powered their world became localized in significant natural features, such as unusual rock formations or streams and lakes. Offerings would be left – perhaps the heavily antlered skull of a red deer – and the first stages of monumentalizing landscapes had begun.

Locales might have remained sacred for many generations, but the way they were monumentalized was ephemeral in nature. Wooden posts, simple shelters for deities, the remains of feasting, and the deposition of bones or hides of sacrificed animals might be all that marked a sacred locale. Nonetheless, such landscapes would have been important not only in their time, but also in providing the model for landscapes that would be monumentalized with great stones by future generations. The megalithic and earthen monuments of the early Neolithic are of great importance as they are not only a direct insight into the shamanic practices of their age but potentially reflect the mindscapes of earlier generations. Evidence that the earthen long barrows and causewayed enclosures of the early Neolithic inspired the megalithic structures of the late Neolithic and the early Bronze Age is found everywhere. The evidence for the link with the shamanic hunter-gatherer communities of the Mesolithic is also present in the design of the first monumental tombs – the earthen long barrows. Earthen long barrows seem to be inspired by the lakeside 'long houses' of the late European Mesolithic. The classic trapezoid shapes of the longhouses found in Poland and Denmark are mirrored in the timber-built earth houses of the dead. Even the post-holes of the internal timber burial chambers reflect the structural form of the houses of the living in late Mesolithic times. [6]

The Mesolithic Community of Star Carr (8,000 BCE)

The surviving material culture of the British Mesolithic consists largely of the product of flint-working and non-ritual food deposits in the form of shell-middens. Evidence for shamanic practices is therefore thin – some would argue non-existent except, as already argued, as a predication from living hunter-gatherer cultures, such as the Tungus of Siberia. There is one substantial exception. One of the most significant Mesolithic locales in archaeological terms is Star Carr, in Yorkshire, where excavations began more than fifty years ago. Its significance lies in the fact that the wet conditions of this ten thousand year old occupation site have preserved much organic material and given a much fuller insight into the lives of these ancient people. [7]

Interpreting Shamanic Landscapes

Star Carr lies at the eastern end of the Vale of Pickering, between the Chalk Wolds of the East Riding and the Limestone Hills of the North Riding of Yorkshire. This was the site of an ancient lake, long since vanished, on whose shores these ancient hunters gathered, made tools, fished and butchered their kill of deer, elk, ox and pig. The culture of the time is referred to as 'Maglemosian' after the famous excavation site at Maglemose on the Danish island of Zealand, where the archaeological finds were to define the distinctive culture of the early Mesolithic. These were the people who re-colonized those tracts of northern lands that had been previously buried under great sheets of ice that covered much of the northern hemisphere during the Devensian cold stage, which lasted between 80,000 and 10,000 years ago.

The environment of the British Mesolithic could hardly be closer to that of the Siberian forests and tundra. This was a world of dense forests, formed as the ice of the last glaciation retreated, in what the archaeologists refer to as the Boreal period of post-glacial climate. This was a primordial world of dank forest and bog, where hunting would focus on the sides of rivers, lakes and forest clearings, where grazing animals might gather. The people of the Mesolithic would have followed migratory routes, defined by their ancestors, that would have utilized fishing and hunting in season, pretty much as the Siberian hunters subsist to this day. In the case of the British Mesolithic, the culture seems to be largely coastal in nature (Star Carr is 6 miles from the sea) and hunting in the forests during the winter months was combined with fishing and gathering shellfish on the beaches during the summer. The barbed antler fishing point is one of the classic signifiers of the Maglemosian culture.

Excavation of the site at Star Carr revealed a man-made lakeside platform, constructed on top of the muddy gravels out of birch tree trunks and branches, lumps of clay and glacial pebbles. The evidence for occupational activity lay primarily in the remains of flint-knapping, barbed antler points and the remains of antler working and butchered animals. The occupation area appears to have been no more than 220 square metres. These were tiny communities – no more than extended family groups - and the pattern seems to have been matched throughout Western Europe. Population expansion did not happen until the agrarian and pastoral economies of the Neolithic made it possible for the land to support much larger populations. At Star Carr, red and roe deer appeared to form the main staple of their diet. With most of their tools made out of antler, deer also dominates their tool assemblage. The occupation platform at Star Carr was a place of intense activity in terms of the fabrication of tools, food preparation and animal hide processing.

The densely wooded environments of the Mesolithic could only support scattered, small populations of perhaps a handful of related families for quite large areas. Occupation sites were temporary. The evidence points, however, to the return to

Interpreting Shamanic Landscapes

favourite sites year after year, thus establishing pathways that would have become sanctified by the presence of forest spirits and the resting places of the dead.

Cultural parallels with living shamanic communities do not, alone, support the presence of the shaman at Star Carr. The critical evidence for his presence lies in how we choose to interpret a number of highly significant artifacts from the animal remains. It is the presence of stag skulls, modified for wearing, that has led to speculation about the religious beliefs and practices of the people of Star Carr.

Grahame Clark, the archaeologist responsible for Star Carr's excavation, described the twenty-one 'worked stag frontlets' as the most remarkable objects from the site. A stag frontlet basically consists of the frontal part of a stag skull, to which is attached the remains of the antlers. The nasal and basal parts of the skull had been broken away, so that only the antler carrying part of the skull remains. Each of these antler frontlets has features in common, including the perforation of the skulls with two holes. The interiors of the skulls had been worked to provide a relatively smooth interior and the sides of the skull removed to make a kind of cap. The perforations would have made it possible to attach the frontlet to something else, so that they could be worn. Clark outlines the evidence that the frontlets had indeed been modified so they could be worn as 'a kind of mask or head-dress'.

"...For one thing great trouble was taken to lighten the antlers...the antlers on the frontlets were reduced to something like a third or a quarter of their weight by the elaborate process of attenuation and hollowing of beams and tines already described.... Secondly, there are signs of special treatment of the rim and parts of the inner surface of the brain case, designed apparently to remove or reduce inequalities and prominent protuberances.... These features, it is submitted, are most easily accounted for on the hypothesis that the frontlets were intended to be worn on the head." [8]

Representations of dancing figures wearing animal masks are known from upper Paleolithic times in Europe, so we may be seeing evidence of the continuation of a tradition going back many thousands of years. The famous so-called 'Sorcerer' of the Sanctuary at the Les Trois Freres cave in the Ariege wears antlers. It is interesting that the stag antler working techniques of the Star Carr community have much in common with those used by the Magdalenian culture that produced the cave paintings in the Sanctuary. We thus have evidence of possible links between the people of Star Carr and the cultures of the Upper Paleolithic that produced such beautiful cave art and created their ritual spaces in the depths of the earth. [9]

Clark cites the many instances of antlers being associated with burials, both of men and women, and the continuation of their association with burials into

Interpreting Shamanic Landscapes

British Bronze Age contexts. One of the strongest explanations, he suggests, is an association with fertility – what we might call sexual magic. Antlered deities even continue into the Celtic period – notably Cernunnos, who is famously depicted on a panel of the Gundestrup bowl from Jutland. He too wears stylized red-deer antlers.

Old engraving of Tungus Shaman

More significantly for our argument, Clark refers to an early illustration (1705) of a Siberian Tungus shaman, beating his drum. The illustration clearly shows the shaman wearing a frontlet identical to those produced by the people of Star Carr. It is likely that this shamanic activity, where the shaman assumes the garb of the stag or deer, is connected with the shaman's function in assuring success in the hunt. The wearing of hide and antlers and the mimicking of the deer in the ecstatic dance would have facilitated the 'capture' of the soul of the deer as a precursor to success in the hunt. It is also possible that the use of stag antlers was connected with fertility. If this is the case, the shaman's role will still be to possess the soul of the stag to ensure success in his mating activities.

The significance of donning the skin and antlers of the stag should not be underestimated as a dimension of shamanic practice. It is the means by which the shaman, in his trance, *becomes* the animal. Mircea Eliade discusses its significance, not just for shamans, but also for 'primitive' cultures in general:

Stag Frontlet from Starr Carr excavations

"We must not forget that the relations between the shaman (and indeed "primitive man" in general) and animals are spiritual in nature and of a mystical intensity that a modern, desacralized mentality finds it difficult to imagine. For primitive man, donning the skin of an animal was becoming that animal, feeling himself transformed into an animal. We have seen that, even today, shamans believe they can change themselves into animals."[10]

In some tribes, Eliade states, the cap, or headdress of the shaman is the most important part of his costume and in it the shaman's power is considered to reside. Curiously, however, the stag horns are

Shamanism and Sacred Landscapes

Interpreting Shamanic Landscapes

often imitated in iron, because of the special power that shamans believe iron contains. Amongst the Tungus shamans, headdresses imitating stag horns are the most common. [11]

Eliade goes on to argue that shamanic ecstasy could be obtained by the "choreographic imitation of an animal." [12]

As I pointed out in chapter 3, sacred or 'magical' theatre involves not just the wearing of masks, but the actor *becoming* the thing he represents. So it was with the mimetic dances of our Mesolithic ancestors, who became the stag in order to draw on his sexual power and to influence the outcome of the hunt.

Some questions regarding the stag frontlets remain unanswered. Why were there so many sets of frontlets? Twenty-one sets, in all, survived. Given the amount of hollowing out of the skull itself and of the antler beams and tines, they involved too much labour simply to use and discard – although some appear to have antler parts re-used, perhaps after sustaining damage. It would seem more likely, that several people participated in the ritual together, perhaps involving ritual combat between 'dancers'. Thus, several participants assumed the shaman's role in the stag dances.

Supportive evidence for this is provided by research carried out over the past century with the San Bushmen of southern Africa, who are described in the chapter on rock art. Reports dating from the nineteenth century and the 1950s show that not one, but half the men and a third of the women of a community were regarded as ritual specialists and took part in large 'medicine' dances. The 'trance-dancing' of the San bush people were connected with animal spirits to guide the antelope herds. We may speculate that similar large-scale participation in trance dancing or other shamanic activities connected with the hunt may explain the large number of antler frontlets at Star Carr. [13]

Without doubt, the evidence for the practice of shamanism during the Mesolithic period of our prehistory remains a matter of interpretation. Nonetheless, the archaeological record and comparisons with shamanic cultures that survived into living memory provide sufficient evidence to support this interpretation.

3.3. Shamanism and Landscape today. Comparisons with the Khanty of Siberia

Many academics regard Siberia as the homeland of what might truly be called 'shamanism'. Shamanism has persisted in Siberia until the present day, providing opportunities for anthropologists and experts in religion to research its practice. The long, dark years of Stalinist Russia saw attempts to eradicate shamanism. Stalin failed, but changing lifestyles and changing landscapes are

Interpreting Shamanic Landscapes

bringing the Time of the Shaman to a close even here. Only in the forests and remote steppes of Siberia, where, the industrial complexes, oil pipelines, and pollution have not yet reached, has the shaman and his primordial world survived intact. Here, semi-nomadic communities continue to subsist by hunting, using age-old skills to survive in a harsh and shrinking world.

The archaeology of shamanism must, perforce, draw upon the evidence of living traditions to make its case. The bedrock of good archaeology is scrupulously accurate recording of what the trowel unearths, followed by its full and accurate publication. Drawing conclusions about what the archaeology actually tells us about our ancestor's beliefs is another matter. Semi-nomadic hunter-gatherers around the world may give us a window into our own past by enabling us to study the kind of material culture and 'archaeological record' living shamanism produces.

Shamanism is not just about an individual attaining ecstasy. His witness to the reality of the otherworld is an affirmation of a world-view that affects every aspect of the life of the community he serves. His vision is the vision of his community. This vision has the potential not only to influence how a landscape is perceived but also the shaping of the landscape itself by the people who move through it. Amongst hunter-gatherer communities, the impact on the landscape in physical terms is necessarily slight. Nonetheless, it has the potential to shed some light on our own past, when we too wandered the forests in a post-glacial world.

In his essay 'The materiality of shamanism as a 'world-view': Praxis, artifacts and landscape.' Peter Jordan [14] explores the beliefs, material culture and perceptions of physical and spiritual landscapes amongst the Khanty, a semi-nomadic community that subsists by hunting in modern Siberia. Jordan explains how the practice of shamanism in such communities is part of a wider belief in a spirit world that impacts on many aspects of daily life. The ecstatic experience of the shaman is but one manifestation of that belief. Jordan's study explores how the beliefs of such communities are manifested in terms of their perceptions of landscape and use of sacred locales within the landscape.

Jordan describes the world-view of the shaman as a 'socially sanctioned cosmology', including a three-tiered view of the cosmos in which the everyday landscapes of communal life play an essential part. The landscape is itself adapted, both in the way it is perceived by the Khanty and in the making of small 'monuments' and depositions, to reflect the presence of the spirit worlds as a 'proximate dimension to human activity'.

The Khanty believe that anything that has the power to breathe, transform, or move has *lilenky*, or soul. Thus, the fast-flowing stream has a soul. Even an inan-

Interpreting Shamanic Landscapes

imate object, such as a rock, may have a soul if a spirit or god has settled in it. Rivers become part of that sacred geography and the 'mighty River Ob' is described by the Khanty as flowing northwards through the middle world of men, before draining downwards into the lower world. This lower world is populated by the dead and is located in the cold, northerly regions, into which the main Siberian rivers drain, taking the souls of the dead with them.[15]

The shaman is only part of the picture of this traffic with the dead, although he alone can journey between the worlds. Feasting and deposition as ritual acts is something in which the entire community participates as part of the seasonal round of hunting activity. Such rituals underpin their vision of the world, with a middle world occupied both by humans and a vast well of souls beyond and just out of sight, who have the power to affect the lives of men for better or worse. Within the Khanty community, the shaman is "at the narrow apex of a much larger 'cone' of communication" with the spirit world.[16]

In the Khanty communities, the basic role of the shaman is healing fractured relationships with the spirit world. He would deal with either the loss or theft of a soul or with the invasion of the soul by an illness bearing spirit. At times of more general social distress, as, for example, when the community is threatened with famine, the shaman would be expected to contact the spirits who control the food supplies. Thus, the shaman is part of a culture in which communication with the spirit world is embedded in the day-to-day activities of the community as a whole. Such communication takes place in a landscape in which the presence of powerful spirits and the souls of the dead are part of everyone's perceptual map. This perceptual map becomes translated, over time, into material depositions within the landscape that may leave an archaeological trace.

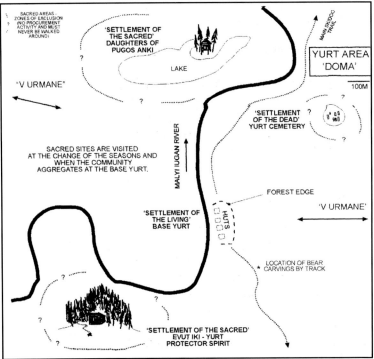

Map of khanty sacred landscape (after Peter Jordan)

Over the generations, a clear settlement pattern has developed amongst the Khanty, including a 'settlement of the dead' – a yurt cemetery, down river from the main 'settlement of the living', situated on the forest edge on

Interpreting Shamanic Landscapes

the banks of the Malyi Iugan river. (The term yurt is used to define a community). Each tract of land has its local 'earth house', where the forest spirit, *Wuhnt Lung*, resides, and offerings are left when entering the area to hunt. These 'earth houses' are often on island groves surrounded by open bog. Making offerings to the forest spirit is vital to ensure the success of the hunt.

Interaction with spirits takes a number of forms. Of significance for the archaeology of shamanism are acts of deposition, where offerings are left in specific locales. These offerings include elk heads, cloth, coins, and vodka. There is also the routine observance of taboos, including using specific routes through the landscape and the avoidance of taboo areas. Ritual meals may be eaten in locales associated with spirits, with the consequent deposition of feasting remnants. [17]

In addition to these 'settlements of the sacred', the Khanty believe that the souls of the dead live on after death in the cemetery – the settlement of the dead. The cemeteries are visited at special times in order to hold special remembrance feasts, a time for communion with dead relatives. If the dead are comfortable in the cemetery there is less chance that their unsettled souls will wander back to the living community at night. After one of the periodic visits to the cemetery, the path is closed symbolically with felled saplings and at other times is strictly avoided. Peter Jordan states that each *yurt* community has its own cemetery, often located downstream, but never upstream from the base *yurt* for fear that 'the diseases of the dead will contaminate the living.'

What this demonstrates is that the Khanty, like the Sora of Orissa, move through a landscape overlaid with a complex spiritual map. The spirit world is 'out there', inextricably interwoven with the visible world. The locales that belong to the spirits are clearly defined and avoided unless it is necessary to do business with the dead. Only certain routes can be used to approach these locales and these have to be ceremonially opened and closed.

Within the British context, it is apparent that many sacred locales, including Stonehenge and Avebury were initially monumentalized with simple structures of earth and timber. The communities who built them would have herded animals, planted grain in season, but still practiced a lifestyle not far removed from the hunter-gatherer. It is possible that the monuments we see today model an arrangement of landscapes of the living, the dead and the powerful spirits that were once perceived within the natural landscape, as indeed is still the case with the Khanty today. At Avebury, we find that the pre-eminent locale for the ancestral dead appears to have been at West Kennett long barrow and at the so-called Sanctuary at Overton Down, where the archaeological remains point to a mortuary structure. These monuments of the dead are situated *downstream* from the ceremonial complexes at Avebury and Windmill Hill and what we may presume were the main sites of the activities of the living. It may be argued that

Interpreting Shamanic Landscapes

the great stone circles and avenues of the later building phases of the Avebury landscape reflect a spiritual and largely conceptual 'map' of earlier generations.

If we apply these same principles to the cursus monuments of ancient Britain, or indeed to the stone rows and processional avenues, we may speculate that their purpose is not just to contain the physical experience of those participating in ritual, but also to contain the dead themselves. Cursus monuments and stone rows define the movement of the living in and out of these places of spiritual power and danger. Likewise, the movement of the Khanty to and from these spiritual 'hotspots' is defined and contained by their use of specific paths and the closing of paths using felled saplings.

The sealing of tombs is not just an act of protecting the bones of the ancestors. It is also designed to prevent the dead from wandering abroad and doing mischief. It is an inevitable consequence of a belief in the power of the dead that the policy towards them is one of containment, as well as intercession and inclusion through shamanic ritual. Within shamanic communities all members of the community have some part to play in their relationships with the spirits, be they spirits of the ancestors, animals or natural phenomena. The role of the shaman is specifically that of trouble-shooter, who because of his ability to cross the divide between the worlds of the living and the dead can do what other men cannot do. Sacred landscapes in the British context demonstrate this communal sense of liminality, where the great temples of the Neolithic and the Early Bronze Age were set up to sanctify places where the world of the living and the dead, of gods and men, meet. The henge – the ditch and bank that surround many of our stone circles, the quarry ditches of earthen long barrows and the banks of cursus monuments all serve to define and contain space in an age when the creation of barriers in any context was a novelty.

The Khanty leave a variety of offerings to the spirits, in the form of ritual deposits. Acts of deposition are found in many archaeological contexts where evidence for ritual feasting is associated with human remains. Of particular significance are the so-called 'causewayed camps', which were built in the early Neolithic. They derive their name from the 'causeways' that interrupt the usually circular ditches and banks that are the main feature of their construction. At Windmill Hill, the causewayed camp near Avebury a most significant assemblage of broken pots and bones, both human and animal, was excavated in the 1930s. Broken pottery is a feature of so many mortuary assemblages of the British Neolithic that it is churlish to suggest that it can have any other meaning than that of an offering to the dead, where the transfer to the otherworld is effected by the destruction of the offering. Similarly, the deposition of feasting remains is also important. In numerous shamanic cultures, the bones of the feast must be returned to the earth or deposited at a sacred locale, both as an offering and because the indestructible soul resides in the bones. The

Interpreting Shamanic Landscapes

placation of the spirit of the slaughtered animal and its eventual return in incarnate form is made possible by the planting of the 'seed' bones in the earth.[18]

The material and spiritual culture of the British Mesolithic would have survived for some time into the Neolithic phase of our prehistory. The peoples of the beach and the forest would have gradually adapted to the ways of the herdsman and the seasonal planter of crops. The making of pottery and the polishing of axes would become a part of their repertoire of skills and some of the old ways would begin to die. New religious beliefs would arise too, connected with the harsh seasonal reality of feast and famine that dependency on a planted crop and the feeding of domesticated animals brings. What is the role of the shaman in these changing times? Can we hear his voice amidst the great stones that our farming ancestors set up to define their relationship with the gods?

What the Khanty may offer us is evidence of the link between the ways that Mesolithic hunter-gatherers 'mapped' their landscapes and the monumentalizing of those landscapes by future generations during the Neolithic. The individual depositions created by shamanic activity are slight, but the larger 'map' divides vast tracts of forest and river into the abodes of spirits and the realms of the living and dead. We may speculate that such mental maps were passed on from generation to generation during the Mesolithic, to be 'written' in the creation of stone monuments in due time. It was no longer sufficient merely to 'imagine' or visualize the division of sacred and profane, but it became necessary to actualize that dualistic vision of the world in monuments of earth and stone.

3.4. Houses for the Dead – the Earthen Long Barrow.

The building of tombs on a vast scale, involving substantial investments of labour, began with the Neolithic or New Stone Age. The crossover between the Mesolithic and the Neolithic is marked by the arrival of techniques of planting cereals, pottery making, and animal husbandry. The planting of cereal crops, the greatest revolution in human history, created food surpluses that powered the building of tombs that remain impressive to this day. The Neolithic cultures of Atlantic Europe provide more evidence of shamanic culture than the great civilizations that evolved elsewhere during the same period of human prehistory. Western Europe retained practices that had been pushed to the edges of society in the great, centralized civilizations of the Nile, Tigris and Euphrates. It was once argued that our Neolithic culture was a debased form of the cultures of Egypt and the Near East. It may well be the case that a slow diffusion of ideas and populations brought cereal-growing from the Near East, where it flourished for thousands of years before coming to Western Europe. Carbon dating and dendrochronology have shown, however, that many of our megalithic tombs pre-date the pyramids. The great tomb of Newgrange, with its quartz

Interpreting Shamanic Landscapes

façade and magnificent corbel roofed burial chamber was already several hundred years old when the first pyramid rose from the desert sand at Saqqara. We should look to the shaman, not the priests of Amun, to explain the religious architecture of the British Neolithic. [19]

The movement of artifacts, such as jadeite axes, from the continent to Britain and the similarity in Neolithic rock art and tomb design from the Danish coast to Southern Spain leaves little doubt that religious ideas, as well as technologies, were communicated along the Atlantic seaboard during the Neolithic. In Eastern Europe, where Neolithic cultures were established at least a thousand years earlier than in Western Europe, we find a distinctive representational art in the form of clay idols in which the Goddess features prominently. In contrast, the artwork found on pottery and carved stones along the Atlantic seaboard is rarely representational. We recognize some of the distinctive geometrical patterns – lozenges, chevrons, spirals, which are also found in Eastern Europe but it offers flimsy evidence for a 'Goddess' culture. In Western Europe, the emphasis on the construction of great tombs is evidence, rather, for a Cult of the Dead, with its attendant need for shamans. [20]

The earliest surviving large-scale monuments from the British Neolithic are known as 'Earthen Long Barrows'. In form they are long, low, trapezoid mounds, sometimes as much as a hundred metres in length, bounded by quarry ditches, which provided the material for the barrow construction. They often contained a small chamber of wood in which the ancestral bones were deposited. Post-hole evidence indicates that some had grand entrance facades, possibly decorated with totem animals, such as the skulls of cattle. Some appear to have had retaining walls of logs. Comparisons with the foundations of longhouses, built on the European mainland in the late Mesolithic, demonstrate that these 'Houses of the Dead' were probably based on an already archaic form of domestic dwelling. In his book, 'The Earthen Long Barrow in Britain', Paul Ashbee explains the links between long barrows and wooden domestic structures of an earlier, Mesolithic time:

"The pitched and turf-built mortuary houses might ultimately owe something to the Circumpolar cultures for houses recalling these forms were widespread amongst the hunting and collecting groups beyond the margin of the temperate forest." [21]

Few of these once great monuments remain as prominent features in the landscape. Most have been ploughed out of existence and survive only as crop marks, visible from the air during periods of drought. A few fine examples have survived, such as Adam's Grave, near Avebury, which was built on the crest of a hill. Others have survived because their remains were incorporated into later Megalithic Long Barrows, or are in isolated locations that have not been subject to the plough.

Interpreting Shamanic Landscapes

Reconstruction of Fussell's Long Barrow (after Paul Ashbee)

Excavations reveal that the earthen long barrow was often not the first, nor the final resting-place of the ancestral dead. In nearly all instances the dead were reduced to bones *prior* to final burial in the barrow. This practice is called excarnation. The evidence lies in the disarticulation of the bones, which are usually placed in the tomb in heaps, and the absence of complete skeletons. In fact, many individuals appear to be represented by only a few fragments of bone – perhaps a skull and a couple of long bones. The state of some bones indicates that the dead were either exposed on platforms or had been previously buried elsewhere in order for the flesh to rot from the bones. The first farmers did not seek to preserve individual identity beyond the grave. Tombs were communal and bones were commingled so that the Ancestor became a common heritage and the tomb a statement of an eternal continuum. Death was the point in which the individual was drawn back into union with the ancestors and the illusion of personality so assiduously created in life was lost forever. The practice of excarnation – leaving the bodies to rot in the open air - makes no mystery of the process of decay. As with the Parsee 'Towers of Silence', the dead are exposed for the birds to take their fill. The body is the cage of the soul and its destruction brings final release. Only the bones survive, to return to the confluence of all life and provide the seed for Nature's endless regeneration.

One famous example of an earthen long barrow is Fussell's Lodge in Wiltshire, excavated by Paul Ashbee in the late 1950s. Despite being reduced by ploughing to a very low, chalky mound, Ashbee was able to rescue both the original grand design and the deposits of ancestral bones, placed within the mound

Shamanism and Sacred Landscapes

Interpreting Shamanic Landscapes

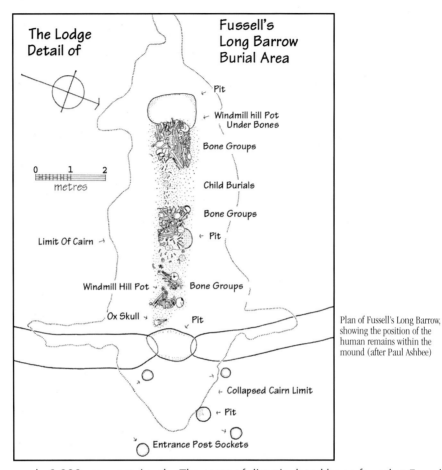

Plan of Fussell's Long Barrow, showing the position of the human remains within the mound (after Paul Ashbee)

nearly 6,000 years previously. The mass of disarticulated bone found at Fussell's Lodge offers some evidence for a long period of exposure to the elements prior to burial in a single act of final internment. Ashbee argued that some of the skeletal remains were already of considerable antiquity at the time of reburial. This opens up the possibility that a number of generations of ancestral remains were reburied in a single, great, reverential act of collective burial. [22]

Fussell's lodge is unusual in containing the bones of over fifty individuals. Often the bone deposits in earthen long barrows are slight. It is possible that they were a token representation of the ancestors, who had been brought from mortuary enclosures or burial grounds elsewhere. There is evidence to show that 'flat' graves were sometimes marked with substantial posts, possibly so that the bones could be located for reburial in due course.

Posthole remains indicate that some earthen long barrows were built over 'mortuary enclosures', used in 'first burial'. We may envisage a palisaded space,

Interpreting Shamanic Landscapes

constructed as an oblong of stout posts, sometimes fronted by a ceremonial courtyard, which was used to contain the dead during cremation or excarnation. Once its ritual life was deemed complete the enclosure was buried under a huge, elongated mound of earth. A good example of this is the Sanctuary, at Avebury, and possibly Woodhenge, close to Stonehenge, where concrete posts now mark where these most ancient of sacred monuments once stood. The earliest significant monumentalizing of the landscape, therefore, is entirely connected with a Cult of the Dead. [23]

It is relevant that our Neolithic forbears invested time and energy, not only in the building of such monuments, but in processes that involved an ongoing relationship with the bones of their ancestors. There is substantial evidence to support the idea that there was movement of human remains from the tombs to nearby gathering places. Bones are clearly regarded as powerful. Shamans generally believe in the power that lies in bones, both animal and humans. It is customary in some shamanic cultures to make use of bones as 'powerfacts'. Eliade refers to the importance of skeletons in a number of contexts. A shaman's costume, for example often incorporate certain iron objects imitating bones, tending, at least partially, to give the appearance of a skeleton. This reflects the belief that the shaman cannot have power until he has experienced, in trance state, the flesh being stripped off his bones, so that he may contemplate his own skeleton:

"By thus seeing himself naked, altogether freed from the perishable and transient flesh and blood, he consecrates himself, in the sacred tongue of the shamans, to his great task, through that part of his body which will longest withstand the action of the sun, wind and weather, after he is dead." Quoted from Rasmussen, describing the shamans of the Iglulik Eskimos. [24]

Many religions, including Hinduism and Tibetan Buddhism, as well as hunter-gatherer communities, regard the stripping of flesh from bone as a requirement to liberate the soul as a precursor to a new life. Eliade states that the reverential treatment of bones applies to both humans and animals in communities where shamanism is practiced. As he states, the soul is presumed to reside in the bones.

" Now, among hunting peoples bones represent the final source of life, both human and animal, the source from which the species is reconstituted at will. This is why the bones of game are not broken, but carefully gathered up and disposed of according to custom, that is, buried, placed on platforms or in trees, thrown into the sea and so on. From this point of view, the burial of animals exactly follows the method used for disposing of human remains. For in both cases alike, the "soul" is presumed to reside in the bones and hence the resurrection of the individual from its bones can be expected." The reduction to a mere skeleton, then, is the path to power for the shaman. [25]

Interpreting Shamanic Landscapes

Shaman ancestors are often directly involved in the initiation of a shaman.[26] In the aboriginal traditions of Australia one becomes a medicine man by sleeping on an ancestral grave.[27] Some Australian tribes initiate their medicine men by leaving them, tied up, in a cemetery for several nights. The ancestral beings encountered in these terrifying ordeals are believed to be responsible for the symbolic death, dismemberment, reconstitution and resurrection of the initiate. The bones of ancestors may indeed be used directly as part of shamanic ritual.[28]

The evidence of Britain's Long Barrows and the skeletal remains found at ceremonial centres, such as Windmill Hill and the Sanctuary, near Avebury, point to the practice of excarnation and use of ancestral bones from the earliest days of the Neolithic. By implication, we may consider that similar practices existed during the Mesolithic in Britain, but ancestral bones were not, at this stage in our prehistory, subjected to secondary burial in monumental tombs and have therefore not survived.

The symbolic deposition of a relatively small quantity of human bone, usually representing several individuals, needs some interpretation. They may have represented the 'gatekeepers' – the ancestral dead whose role it was to link the world of the living with the Otherworld. Likely candidates for such a role would be the shamans, who, in death, would continue to serve their community as they had in life.

It was once popular amongst archaeologists to regard the earthen long barrows as territorial markers, or 'symbols of power', in which a claim to territory and a manifestation of the power of a clan was expressed by building impressive monuments to house the ancestors. Increasingly it is being recognized that there is no transparent link between such monuments and permanent settlements. At the time that earthen long barrows were being constructed the builders continued with a semi-nomadic, pastoral lifestyle. Research indicates that cereal cultivation was comparatively rare in the early Neolithic and relationships between cultivated areas and long barrow construction cannot be established as a pattern. It is more likely that they served as meeting grounds for ceremonial occasions and festivals, and were sited at locales already held as sacred. The primary reason for their construction was religious and ritualistic. Chris Tilley suggests they have a relationship with ancient paths, and places in the landscape that already possessed symbolic or ritual significance.

At some stage in their history, the majority of these tombs were deliberately sealed. In the case of the earthen long barrow, this was accomplished by burning the wooden chamber, filling the chamber with earth or deliberately collapsing the roof.[29] What prompted this final sealing of tombs is not known. At West Kennett Long Barrow, the sealing was completed with huge blocking stones that were clearly designed to create an impressive ritual space in front of the now sealed tomb. It is presumed that ceremonies continued at West Kennet long after its final closing. Indeed, many Long Barrows, such as that at Belas Knap, had grand, false entrances built as part of their initial design. Sealed or open, we may presume that these ceremonial spaces were the point of communication with the spirit world. When the shaman of old danced and drummed it was surely here he entered his trance state, before passing through the portals that divide the worlds of the living and the dead.

3.5. Feasts for the Living and the Dead – Causewayed Enclosures

Contemporary with the building of Long Barrows, and often built close by, was a type of monument now referred to as 'causewayed enclosures. Archaeologists generally believe these were multi-functional meeting places. Some may have even been defensive. There is also substantial evidence to support their role in rituals connected with the ancestors and hence with shamanism. Causewayed Enclosures are a ceremonial or communal space, constructed by enclosing an area of land. They are roughly circular spaces, contained within banks and ditches of earth and rubble. Causeways break the banks and ditches – usually several of them – allowing access to the central space. The evidence indicates that the causeways were an important aspect of the design.[30] The accompanying palisades also appear to have been interrupted. The mystery lies in the fact that the causeways make it difficult to understand the function of the enclosures. The causeways would make them harder to defend and limit their use in containing livestock. The banks and ditches would appear to be a symbolic boundary defining what must have been ceremonial or sacred space. They are the first attempts to enclose large amounts of land and they indicate a changing perception of the natural world. What Nature has given is altered. What is shared by all life is now possessed by a few. The ditch and bank is liminal, separating the sacred from the profane.

Some have argued for a defensive function for the causewayed enclosure, but this is not borne out by the archaeological evidence in the case of the early examples. The fact that the ditch is on the *inside* of the bank argues against defence, where a raised bank would clearly give an attacker an advantage. In hillforts the ditch is on the *outside*.[31]

The many ritual deposits, of what appears to be animal sacrifice, feasting and deposition of human remains is evidence, rather of a ritual function, amongst many other functions the causewayed enclosure must have served.[32]

Possibly, the causeways represent the evolution of the concept of land ownership. The land is enclosed but open so that all may wander freely in and out.

Interpreting Shamanic Landscapes

But we have 'altered the earth', thus setting upon it a mark by which we will be remembered. The creation of such monuments indicates that our separation from Nature has already happened inside our heads. They mark both the zenith of the shaman and the beginning of his decline.

Causewayed enclosures are a dimension of the early Neolithic. They often remained in use for long periods of time. But they did not simply disappear. The causewayed enclosure seems to have evolved into what is generally referred to as the 'henge' monument. Instead of multiple causeways, the henge is often defined by only two entrances, which may or may not have celestial alignments. They consist of a circular bank of earth or rubble on the outside, a berm or flat area, and then a ditch. The significant feature is that the ditch is on the inside, meaning that it was almost entirely unsuited for defence (the attacker would have the higher ground), and therefore we must look to a ritual function for these monuments. Stonehenge itself appears to have begun life in the late Neolithic as a simple 'henge monument, that is, consisting of no more than a circular ditch and bank constructed out of the chalk. The standing stones came later. The respect for these early monuments is evidenced in the fact that so many became a part of Bronze Age ritual landscapes, or, like Stonehenge, continued to evolve as new belief systems and rituals came and went.

Passage and kerb stone, Loughcrew, County Meath, Ireland

3.6. Gateways to the Underworld - Megaliths and Passage Graves

At the height of the Neolithic several differing tomb types were prevalent in the British Isles. Wooden burial chambers gave way to enduring stone. Our ancestors took particular pride in moving enormous megaliths, not only as a religious act, but possibly also as an expression of communal pride and power. Many megalithic tombs are truly awesome, with capstones weighing several tens of tons. They often appear in our landscape as dolmens but this is not how they would have appeared following construction. Most would have been covered with mounds or cairns. In some parts of Britain, such as the so-called 'Severn-Cotswold' region, the tombs remained trapezoid in plan, reflecting the ancient tradition of the earthen long barrow. Elsewhere, possibly influenced by the great Boyne Culture that built Newgrange, they assumed a circular shape, with passages leading to the heart of the tomb. These are referred to as Passage Graves.

Interpreting Shamanic Landscapes

Newgrange passage grave, showing its quartz façade

Gateways to the Underworld

Passage Graves are a classic tomb type of the Western Atlantic Neolithic. The design incorporates a long passage leading to either a single burial chamber or a complex of chambers. These tombs are a kind of sacred theatre in which a *physical* journey is made to a realm of darkness and silence – an environment that may help to induce a *mental* journey, particularly if combined with the consumption of hallucinogenic plants. I have experienced the sensory impact of the utter darkness and silence of the inner chambers of the Maes Howe type passage graves of Cuween Hill and Wideford Hill on Orkney. Those entering the tomb must crawl on hands and knees down a low, narrow passage to the central, corbel roofed chamber. From the central chamber it is a claustrophic squeeze through an even smaller passage to enter the satellite chambers, where the bones of the ancestors were once stored. To be alone in the total darkness and silence of these small chambers is to experience a kind of *conscious death* where the senses strain for some kind of stimulus but receive none. Why the long, deliberately narrow entrance passage to a chamber that is tiny compared with the external size of the monument? Is it meant to replicate a birth or a death experience? To describe the structural elaboration as purely functional is rather like saying the design of a typical Gothic church is purely functional. Both are designed to change the way we experience reality, as well as making a statement about the nature of the cosmos. The passage grave simulates the psychic and physical disintegration in the darkness and silence of the grave. They are a gateway, through which the shaman may travel between the worlds and truly be with the ancestors.

Shamanism and Sacred Landscapes

Interpreting Shamanic Landscapes

The circular plan of the passage grave, with its long, confining entrance is found elsewhere in Neolithic design. In stone circles and henge monuments, it is the circle and causewayed entrance that predominates. The overall plan of passage graves, stone circles, causewayed enclosures and other henge monuments are remarkably similar. This also applies to Neolithic rock carvings. Over 90 % of rock art motifs are circular, being either simple cup marks or cup marks surrounded by concentric rings. [33]

Cup and ring marks and sunbursts, passage grave art Loughcrew, County Meath, Ireland

Why the overwhelming predominance of the circular design? Circular monuments often connect with significant celestial features, as at Newgrange, where the passage is aligned on the Midwinter Solstice dawn, or Maes Howe, which aligns with the Midwinter Solstice sunset. There is a strong argument, stated in the previous chapter, that long barrow design was inspired by the long houses, which were a typical dwelling of late Mesolithic and Neolithic communities in continental Europe. It could be argued that the transition to a circular design marks a similar transition to circular dwellings. Others have argued for a comparison with the roundness of the belly of a pregnant woman, with the passage into the tomb a symbolic representation of the birth passage. My argument against this thesis, as I mentioned previously, is the absence of representations, figurative or otherwise, of 'goddess' figures in the Neolithic cultures of the Atlantic seaboard.

Clearly, Nature played her part in inspiring monumental design. The dome shape of the tomb mirrors the dome of the sky, just as the henge monument mirrors the distant horizon. Circles govern our perception of the world and the celestial bodies manifest themselves as circles too. The transparent reality of those early agriculturists was that their lives were dominated by the changing patterns of the ever-revolving sky. The great mysteries lay above and below them – the power of the heavens to determine events on earth and the power of the earth itself to dissolve the dead and to renew. All three realms of the tripartite world-view – earth, heaven and the world below - are pierced and connected by the invisible polar axis. The axis provides the route for shamanic journeys between the worlds. [34]

Interpreting Shamanic Landscapes

We may imagine a view of the cosmos that is defined by this simple image. The shaman of Siberia defines the cosmos in terms of his tent, which is also circular, and the central pole, which penetrates the earth and reaches up to the sky. This same image is created by the Cosmic Tree, which is climbed in order to ascend to the sky. The Passage Grave reflects these elements. In the world below, the ancestors sleep. The polar axis is symbolized by the passage, which gives access to the world below. At the same time it links with significant aspects of the cosmos, thus linking the world above with the world below.

The defining example of the Passage Grave is Newgrange in County Meath, Ireland. Newgrange is part of a great Neolithic necropolis, built in a wide valley created by a bow-shaped bend in the River Boyne. Amongst the remains of seventy or so passage graves there are three tombs of truly monumental proportions – Dowth, Knowth and Newgrange. Knowth and Newgrange have been restored following excavation and have become Ireland's foremost tourist attractions. In the countryside of County Meath, hundreds of passage graves have survived to speak of a rich 5000-year-old culture, whose people honoured the dead and maintained their relationship with the ancestors through the medium of the tomb.

Kerbstone with spiral designs and entrance to Newgrange passage grave

The passage leading to the heart of the tomb at Newgrange is nearly eighty feet long. The comparable passage of the Knowth tomb, nearby, is over a hundred feet long. Here the shamanic journey to the otherworld is mapped out in stone. We pass over the magnificently carved kerbstone at the great tomb of Newgrange – the barrier that divides the living from the dead – to begin a journey that takes us, quite literally, to the underworld. As you walk toward the heart of the tomb the darkness enfolds completely, for the raised height of the burial chamber and the upward slope of the passage gradually excludes all light from the entrance. At its heart, where the

Shamanism and Sacred Landscapes

Interpreting Shamanic Landscapes

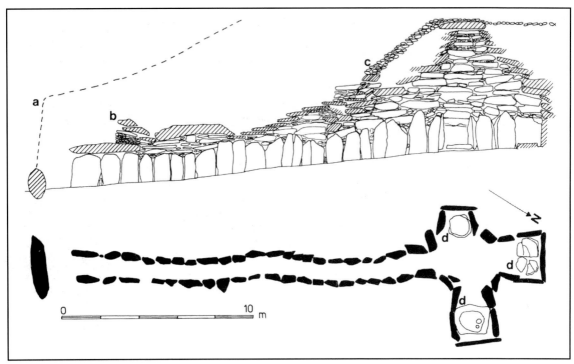

Plan and elevation of the passage into Newgrange (after Michael O'Kelly)

corbelled roof soars upward, are three chambers containing the stone bowls in which the bones of the ancestors lie. The design of the passage creates a physical and spiritual journey from the land of the living to the Court of the Ancestors.

The passage into Newgrange may also be seen as a cosmic axis, uniting the heavens and the underworld. Above the doorway into the tomb is an oblong-shaped opening that became known as the roof box. The purpose of this unique feature was unknown until December 1967 when the excavator of Newgrange, Michael O'Kelly, checked out local stories that a stone in the burial chamber, carved with a triple spiral, was illuminated by the rising sun 'at some unspecified time.' Following a hunch, he discovered that at sunrise on the Midwinter solstice a shaft of sunlight enters the tomb by way of the roof box, and briefly illuminates the entire chamber. He wrote an account of his experiences when he checked his observations in 1969:

"At exactly 8.54 hours GMT the top edge of the ball of the sun appeared above the local horizon and at 8.58 hours, the first pencil of direct sunlight shone through the roof-box and along the passage to reach across the tomb chamber floor as far as the front edge of the basin stone in the end recess. As the thin line of light widened to a 17 cm band and swung across the chamber floor, the tomb was dramatically illuminated and various details of the side and end recesses could be clearly seen in the light reflected from the floor." [35]

Interpreting Shamanic Landscapes

Michael O'Kelly speculates in his chapter on 'The Cult of the Dead' that this feature may not have been unique to Newgrange and the Boyne context. Similar orientations are found in a number of tombs at Loughcrew, Co. Meath and some Breton passage graves.

Some researchers have made specific links between the design of the passage grave and tunnel of light experience commonly encountered in altered states of consciousness. Symbolically, this experience is depicted, according to some archaeologists, in one of the most common forms of rock art – the cup and ring pierced by a single line. This will be discussed at greater length in the chapter on rock art. At this point it is enough to say that this design possibly symbolizes the *actual* journey made into the heart of the passage grave and the *experiential* journey made in the shamanic trance. In effect, the passage grave may have been designed to reflect the experiences of the shaman in his trance state and to provide a physical manifestation of that journey. Put simply, the inspiration for the design of passage graves is a combination of the shamanic worldview and the actual experiences of the shaman whilst in a trance state.

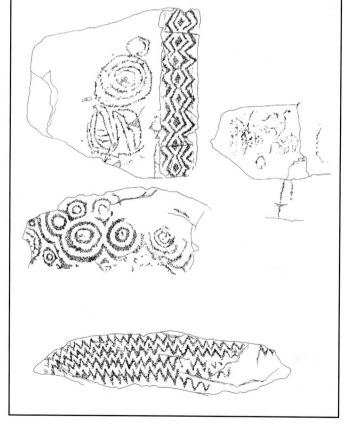

Decorated stones from Fourknocks passage grave, County Meath (after E. Shee Twohig)

Jeremy Dronfield has carried out some research into this concept. He completed his doctoral thesis on 'Subjective visual phenomena in Irish Passage Tomb Art'. His research has been inspired by the similarity in the spiral designs encountered in the art of Neolithic tombs and the 'entoptic' phenomenon of tunnels and vortices experienced in trance states. The word 'entoptic' refers to the visual experiences generated by our brain and optical nervous system in trance states.

Dronfield specific interest lies with the "vortex or tunnel experience" commonly encountered in altered states of consciousness and described in near death experiences. Neurological research suggests the spiral or vortex phenomenon occurs in human beings as a result of spontaneous firing of specific neurons in the medial superior temporal area of the visual cortex. This 'tunnel' experience was also a physically real experience

Shamanism and Sacred Landscapes

Interpreting Shamanic Landscapes

for those charged with bringing the dead down the narrow tunnels to the burial chambers at the heart of the tomb. Dronfield argues that the passage tombs may be an attempt to physically reconstruct a mental journey or experience. Based upon the distribution of the concentric circle and spiral designs, Dronfield concluded that the concentric designs inside the Irish passage tombs were not simply representations of passages but "signified the locations of points of access to other worlds." Inside the tomb, the rock carvings often mark significant physical thresholds within the tomb. The famous triple spiral at Newgrange, for example, marks the entrance to the central chamber itself. In Dronfield's view, this made the tombs much more than just bone repositories or places for "ritually enacted communication with the dead." They were places where, through myth, ritual and entering into trance states those engaged in the rituals were able to experience travel between the worlds of the living and the dead.

Richard Bradley working in Orkney, Scotland, has also suggested that the passage grave structure symbolized the journey towards the otherworld and the back stone was the portal, which could only be passed through after death. He not only argues that the spiral motifs found in tombs reflect altered states of consciousness, but also that passage tombs may have been constructed so as to create the conditions under which they might be experienced. [37]

At Newgrange the rock carvings fall into three main groups - the spiral, the chevron and the lozenge. There are also some groups of concentric rings, some cup marks and sunray designs. Most of the other motifs found are variations on these themes. Some of these carvings were executed on the backs of the visible stone surfaces and were concealed forever by the construction process. We may assume that they were meant to confer some kind of power or sanctity to the stones themselves. The carvings on the exterior surfaces, on the other hand, were meant to be 'read' by those approaching the tomb and would have expressed the meaning of the monument for the laity gathering to witness the shaman's journey. The visible carvings that continue *within* the monuments would be visible only to a few. The intended audience might be the priest or shaman, whose direct role it was to communicate with the dead. If Dronfield is correct, these interior carvings were liminal, marking the precise nexus of the worlds of the living and dead and the point of penetration of those about to commence their journey to the other side.

Tripple spiral rock carving at Newgrange

Interpreting Shamanic Landscapes

3.7. The Shamanic Key – The Rock Carvings of Ancient Britain

> " The dreamtime ancestors still exist inside the earth or under the ground, they are 'covered over' and lie beneath the visible physical surfaces of the land. Art applied to the body or to the surfaces of the rocks may, in the context of ceremonies, act so as to 'pull out' ancestral forces.... For these rites to be fully effective they had to take place at the original geographical sites."
>
> *Christopher Tilley*

Rock carvings and rock paintings are our oldest surviving art form. All over the globe ancient cultures have carved and painted designs of one kind or another onto rock surfaces. Rock art may well be humankind's first venture into representing their understanding of the cosmos. Evidence exists to support the claim that some rock art in Australia is over 30,000 years old. In Europe, the work of Paleolithic artists dates back tens of thousands of years. There has been much speculation as to its meaning. The idea that it is in some way connected with magical practices has long been popular. More recently, research into the rock art of the San Bushmen of southern Africa has supported the concept that a great deal of rock art is shamanic in origin. The San Bushmen commemorated what appears to be a journey into the rock itself with rock carvings. In this instance, the use of lines and zoomorphic forms make the meaning transparent. Richard Bradley, reporting the work of Lewis-Williams, comments that:

Rock carvings showing animals apparently entering or emerging from the Otherworld (after Pena)

"Shamans sometimes report the sensation of travelling through the solid rock, entering or leaving through the natural cracks....This can be represented in rock art by lines which extend for many metres through a rock shelter.... Sometimes incomplete animals are depicted, as if they were entering the surface of the stone." [38]

Shamanism and Sacred Landscapes

Interpreting Shamanic Landscapes

In the Galician rock art of Spain, which dates from the Neolithic, animals sometimes appear to be emerging from circles and spirals and in several cases their bodies have been left incomplete, as if part of their form is emerging from or penetrating the rock. What is absent from British rock art are the zoomorphic and anthropomorphic images of the San Bushmen and the Galician Neolithic. In every other way there is a major commonality of style and design.

Rock art occurs in tombs, on standing stones and in the carvings on natural outcrops of rock in the northern regions of the British Isles from Orkney to Anglesey. They are found on living rock in landscapes as far afield as the Kilmartin Glen in the west of Scotland and Ilkley Moor in North Yorkshire. The work of archaeologists such as Peter Jackson and others has suggested that these designs echo the experiences of the shaman and therefore symbolize the religious beliefs of a people. [40] By far the most common form in the British landscape is the so-called 'cup and ring' design and many of the more complex designs are variations on this theme. In the same way that the cross is the symbol that links all things Christian, the classic 'cup and ring' design of rock art might be regarded as the key to the Stone Age soul.

In the past, mainstream archaeologists have been disinclined to risk their careers researching rock art. Dating rock art was difficult because there was little to contextualize it with. It was also problematic in that any attempt to interpret rock art was considered to be purely speculative. There seemed to be no basis for a 'scientific' approach to its study. It was left to the amateur to record the thousands of examples of rock art in the far away places of southern Africa, Australia and North America. In Britain rock art has not attracted the same kind of interest amongst lovers of ancient monuments that stone circles and dolmens have. This is because they are often in out of the way places and difficult to find. They are intimate in nature, requiring close proximity to exert their power. This lack of glamour has perhaps added to the fact that books on rock art don't line the bookshelves as books on stone circles do.

What has changed to make rock art of interest to academics, as well as those interested in shamanism in general?

There have been two major areas of research, which have cast new light on these most enigmatic of sacred monuments. The first was carried out in South Africa in which rock art was interpreted in the light of what early ethnographic research had revealed about the people who made them. Scientific research into the similarity between recurring designs in rock art and images generated by the brain when in a trance state – so-called entoptic phenomena – have further strengthened the argument.

Interpreting Shamanic Landscapes

The Rock Art of San Bushmen and the work of J. D. Lewis-Williams. [41]

Comparing the shaman of today with the remains of our own Mesolithic and Neolithic past is a crude research tool. Nonetheless, some archaeologists are using anthropology and 'living' material landscapes to comment upon the interpretation of surviving material deposition from prehistoric times. In the case of the San Bushmen of Southern Africa, for example, we have the surviving corpus of rock art and a precious resource of late nineteenth century research carried out amongst the San, before the 'living memory' of its meaning disappeared. Verbatim accounts were made which describe the myths, rituals, religious practices and daily lives of the San. It has been possible to tie in the complex mythology and religious beliefs and practices of the San with their rock art. This combination of archaeology and anthropology has led a number of researchers to conclude that San Rock Art is shamanic in origin and purpose. Such research has the potential to shed light on the meaning of British rock art.

The images of San (Bushman) rock art are amongst the most captivating and best understood in the world. There is a huge and well-studied corpus of rock art in Southern Africa from thousands of rock shelters. In the past it was often assumed that the function of all of this art was purely decorative – in other words we made the same assumptions for the San rock art as we make for our own sculptures and paintings.

San Religion and its Social and Conceptual Contexts.

Wilhelm Bleek, a German philologist made a study of San beliefs and practices in the 1870s. In a context where little was known about the religions of small-scale societies, Bleek faithfully recorded what his informants told him, often with little understanding. Much of his work was not published until the 1930s. Bleek's accounts are important because they are contemporary with the painting of the last rock art images.

The San studied by Bleek lived in the semi-arid interior of the southern African plateau. They lived in bands or camps of an average of 25 people. They moved seasonally to exploit scarce food supplies and exploit the scattered waterholes that were liable to dry up or turn brackish in the winter. They hunted with bows and poisoned arrows.

The San believed in a trickster deity known as /Kaggen, which is often translated as 'Mantis'. The San did not worship the mantis insect, but regarded the mantis as one of /Kaggen's many avatars, which included eland, eagles and snakes. The cosmos which /Kaggen and the San inhabited was three-tiered – there were spiritual realms above and below the level on which people lived. The spiritual realms constantly impinged on the lives of people.

Interpreting Shamanic Landscapes

Ritual specialists moved between these realms. They accomplished this by entering an altered state of consciousness in a large 'medicine' dance, in more solitary circumstances or in dreams. Trance was induced not by the taking of hallucinogenic substances, but by intense concentration, prolonged rhythmic dancing, drumming and hyperventilation. In the spirit world they healed the sick of ailments often sent by malevolent spirits of the dead, caused rain to fall, and guided the movements of antelope so that they ran into the hunter's ambush. In the 1950s researchers in the Kalahari found that up to half the men and a third of the women in a San camp were ritual specialists of this kind, and the nineteenth century texts suggest that similar proportions existed in related tribes then. [42]

San myths show that /Kaggen was the original shaman. He created potency and imbued the eland with it. When he created the eland, he was in fact creating the foundation of San shamanism. With the eland, /Kaggen tries to outwit the hunters and to protect the animals. He is thus 'Lord of the Animals' – a common figure in shamanistic communities. The San described how the 'shamans of the game', as they called them, *entered the spirit world* to trick the trickster and to guide antelope herds into the hunter's ambush. Lewis-Williams argues that many of the rock paintings depict out-of-body travel and transformation into animals. The famous eland of San rock art – once regarded as no more than another hunted animal – is now understood as a key symbol of the /Kaggen and hence of San shamanism. [43]

With the growth in understanding of the symbolic roles of the animals depicted in San rock art as the depiction of shamanic rituals it became possible to understand the role of rock art within the context of the San communities. Lewis-Williams argues that shamans who wished to 'fix' their experience for the benefit of the community may have painted many of the rock paintings. As is the case with all shamanic discourse, the depictions, visual or oral, of the shamanic 'journey', is framed by the shared mythology and world-view of the larger community. However abstract or incoherent the experience of the shaman, he or she must integrate his experience into the life of the community within the framework of a shared conceptual landscape.

Rock art is a kind of reservoir of experience and energy that other shamans may tap into. So that rock art could always be 'read', Lewis-Williams argues that the conventions guiding the painting of rock art would have been as defined as the rules governing written language. The symbolism used would therefore have been transparent in meaning to the San community.

Rock art in the British context.

The San experience offers evidence that the creation of rock art reflects the beliefs and religious practices of a shamanic culture. The images painted on the

Interpreting Shamanic Landscapes

rock faces offer an insight both into the mythology of the San, their rituals and their shamanizing. The written record of early ethnographers and the representational nature of much of San rock art facilitate the interpretive process.

The major difference between the rock art of the San and that found in the British context is that British rock art is rarely representational. One has to travel to Spain to find substantial representations of animals in the Neolithic rock art of Europe. Nonetheless, it is clear that the symbolism employed was coherent and used wherever rock art was produced. Other than the consistency of design, what other clues do we have that will help us enter the mindscape of those who carved these stones? I will examine three avenues of enquiry into interpreting rock art, all of which point to the idea that rock art in the British context also served an important role in shamanic practices.

The Nature of the Designs.

The similarities in design across the entire distribution of rock art in Atlantic Europe are striking. The motifs of the so-called 'cup and ring' designs and the various multi-ring variants are perhaps the most common designs. Another common feature are lines radiating out from the cup and rings that may link up with other cup and rings and thus create a unity of design, which appears to conform to certain rules. On rock outcrops and boulders over 90 % of motifs are circular, either simple cup marks or cup marks surrounded by concentric rings. Less than 10% of motifs are based on single, or in combinations of, straight lines. The 'cup and ring' design often features a straight line or 'pathway', which begins on the outside of the series of rings and ends at the cup in the centre of the nest of rings. Where we find rocks with a substantial number of such designs, which range in size and complexity it often appears that they have been produced over a period of time and possibly by several different hands. Within the context of tombs, a much wider corpus of designs is found. Chevrons and lozenges, complex spirals, sunbursts and axe-heads are found. There are also a small number of designs that might be interpreted as anthropomorphic. The composition of such designs, where they cover large surfaces of rock, generally do not appear to form an overall design. The most famous excep-

Carved stone, Fourknocks Passage Grave, County Meath, showing 'entoptic' design

Shamanism and Sacred Landscapes

Interpreting Shamanic Landscapes

tions are kerbstones K1, K52 and K57 at Newgrange, as well as some superbly carved smaller stone slabs at tombs such as Fourknocks in County Meath. For the most part, however, the symbolism seems to be focused on the individual designs, rather than the entire carved surface. [44]

Broadly speaking, there are a number of possible ways to interpret rock art designs in terms of their meaning. These are summarized by Bradley:

"One conceives the motifs as a reflection of routine experience as portrayals, however distant, of features seen in everyday life. A second extends this kind of approach to the evidence of specialised monuments: buildings that might be encountered less frequently and perhaps only on certain occasions. *And the third sees the images as a reflection of states of altered consciousness, experienced at these monuments among other places and mediated through the human nervous system.*" [45]

Bradley suggest they might be interpreted as a kind of spiritual 'map':

"It is well known that certain supposedly abstract paintings created by native Australians are actually conceived as maps, but as maps that depict the movements of mythical beings and show a landscape in which the supernatural permeates every activity." [46]

Bradley's suggestion that these repeated designs might reflect images generated during 'altered states of consciousness' is borne out by research in this area.

Neuropsychological Research on Altered states of Consciousness.

Navicular carvings, kerbstone at Knowth, County Meath, Ireland

Neuropsychological research has now demonstrated that certain types of hallucination are produced by the central nervous system to predictable patterns. These mental images may include zigzags, dots, grids, meandering lines and 'U' shapes. In the literature, they are variously called 'phosphenes' or 'entoptic phenomena'. Entoptic phenomena are often experienced in a comparatively light altered state of consciousness, however that altered state is induced. The range of entoptic forms was established by laboratory experiments involving electrical stimulation of the cortex

Interpreting Shamanic Landscapes

or ingestion of LSD and other hallucinogens. The subjects of the experiment were then asked to draw the visualizations that had been generated. They tended to depict what they had seen in recognizable forms, depicting their visualizations as familiar geometrical shapes. This differs from those who depict their experiences following authentic shamanic experiences. They tend to rearrange their visualizations to match their notions of the spirit world, as is the case with most shamanic experiences in 'believing' communities.

The human central nervous system is identical in all of us and therefore individuals of all cultures are likely to experience similar entoptic phenomena. The parallels with entoptic phenomena and the patterns found in British rock art are striking, almost as if the shaman artist sought to portray his visionary experiences as accurately as he could. Elsewhere in the world figurative paintings and carvings often show a remarkable resemblance to the original abstract forms. The brain seemingly attempts to identify or decode entoptic forms by matching them against conscious experiences. [47]

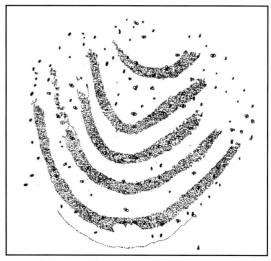

Navicular rock paintings, South Africa – after Pager

Most rock paintings amongst the San Bushmen are figurative. Lewis-Williams argues that the figurative forms in San rock art are attempts to interpret the universal abstract phenomena in terms of San mythology. He gives the example of what are termed 'navicular entoptic phenomena'. This is one of the most widely known entoptic phenomena and consists of a set of curves, nestling one within the other. A more elaborate form involves zigzags. Within these sets of curves and zigzags a black area may appear. This black area may override what the person normally sees, such that part of the normal visual field is obscured. The overall shape is of a curved space containing a black area, which. Lewis-Williams describes as having a boat or 'navicular' shape. The related San rock art ranges from simple, geometrical shapes that appear to reflect the raw 'entoptic' experience all the way through to complex representations of boat journeys and strange anthropomorphic creatures, all of which are amenable to interpretation within the context of San mythology. [48]

Anthropomorphic navicular rock painting, South Africa, – after Lewis-Williams

Interpreting Shamanic Landscapes

Interpreting Cup and Ring Marks in the British Context

The most ubiquitous British rock art design – the cup and ring design – requires more specific interpretation as they appear to link to the visual experiences produced by oxygen deprivation, such as might be produced by hyperventilating, whirling, intense chanting or other shamanic techniques. The cup and ring design has three basic components as I said earlier, these being the cup at the core, any number of encircling rings and a line that cuts through the rings to the cup at the core. The cup, visually, is an area of darkness. When surrounded by rings it gives the impression of a tunnel. Those subjected to oxygen deprivation by whatever means (anything from the effects of a heart attack to the effects of 'G' forces on some airforce pilots) often have the sensation of travelling down a tunnel. Shamanic trance techniques may replicate the same conditions and thus give the effect of journeying into the earth. The line that often breaks the rings and leads to the cup of darkness at the core seems to represent a pathway into the centre.

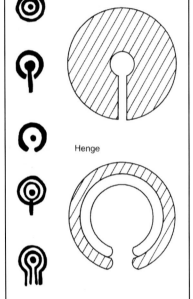

Passage grave and henge plans compared with cup and ring designs (after Richard Bradley)

This may be interpreted as a symbol of a shamanic journey through the rock to the otherworld. At the same time, and of crucial importance in the interpretation of Neolithic tomb architecture, this design appears to provide a blueprint of the interior layout of passages graves. It remains an open question as to which inspired which. It may be that the cup and ring or 'tunnel of light' carvings inspired the layout of passage graves or vice-versa. Whichever way it is, there is a direct link between rock carvings of this kind and a shamanic world-view in which a journey, either in trance or in full consciousness, is made from one world to the next.

It is interesting that cup and ring marks, though ubiquitous on rock surfaces and boulders, are much less common on passage graves, where designs inspired by entoptic phenomena seem to predominate. One argument is that the 'cup and ring' design, as symbol of gateway to the underworld, is no longer necessary when the gateway is present in the physical form of the tomb itself. The cup and ring carving, then, stands in place of the passage to the otherworld.

3.8. Stone Circles, Standing Stones, Wood Henges and the Concept of the Cosmic Tree.

Stone circles generally belong to the later Neolithic and the Bronze Age. Archaeologists have demonstrated that many replaced the timber circles of an earlier age. Stonehenge is an excellent example of a monument that began life as a henge monument with a timber structure in the early Neolithic and was

Interpreting Shamanic Landscapes

transformed several times until it took its final form in the early Bronze Age. Stanton Drew in the Cotswolds, and the Sanctuary at Avebury, have surviving postholes of earlier wood circles, providing evidence of their evolution from Neolithic timber circles to late Neolithic and Bronze Age stone circles. Timber circles preceded many of Britain's stone circles. Hundreds, no doubt, remain to be discovered from posthole evidence. Britain also has the unique instance of the surviving timbers of Seahenge. The inverted tree-bole of Seahenge provides stark evidence of shamanic practice:

One of the surviving stones of 'Nine Stones Close', Harthill Moor

"The Siberian shamans also have their personal trees, which are simply representatives of the Cosmic Tree; some shamans also use "inverted trees," that is, trees planted with their roots in the air, which, as is well known, are among the most archaic symbols of the World Tree." [49]

Timber circles and ritual enclosures provide a possible link with shamanism, as it is known today. Eliade refers to a cosmic tree set within a kind of stockade when he describes the consecration of a machi, a South American shamaness:

"This initiation centres on the climbing of a tree or rather a tree stripped of bark, called a rewe... A nine foot tree is barked, notched to form a ladder, and solidly set in the ground in front of the future shamaness's house, "tilted slightly backwards to make it easier to climb." Sometimes "tall branches are stuck in the ground all around the rewe, forming an enclosure for it of 15 by 4 metres." [50]

That such ritual enclosures existed in the British and Western European Neolithic cannot be doubted. Often they are interpreted as 'mortuary enclosures'. Their use for shamanic ritual seems plausible. Aubrey Burl suggests that the shamans of the timber circles may have evolved to become the priesthood who carried out the great rituals of state in the sacred landscapes of Avebury and Stonehenge. [51]

When we consider the role of such structures in shamanic ritual, we realize that current popular interpretations of wood and stone circles as 'astronomical observatories' or 'calendars' only obscures the intentions of their builders. Stone circles, alignments, and cursus monuments are not astronomical observatories.

Interpreting Shamanic Landscapes

They were stage sets for the enactment of cosmic dramas, just as a Roman Catholic church or a Hindu Temple is today. Astronomical alignments only serve to affirm the relationship of a symbolic enactment by men with the cosmic drama, taking place in the sky. Astronomy was a child of the supernal, not of science. The construction of monuments involves creating ritual spaces in which the numinous may manifest itself in the physical world. The monument completes the circle in which the vision is imposed on the landscape, thus healing the divide between our conscious and unconscious lives - the landscape of the gods and the landscapes of men. The land is transformed by the monument into a shamanic mindscape.

The Cosmic Tree.

The technology of the shaman facilitates the passage from one cosmic region to another – from earth to the sky or from earth to the underworld. The shaman believes that the very structure of the universe makes this possible. The universe is conceived as having three levels – sky, earth, and underworld – connected by a central axis. The axis passes through a hole, or opening:

"It is through this hole that the gods descend to earth and the dead to the subterranean regions; it is through the same hole that the soul of the shaman in ecstasy can fly up or down in the course of his celestial or infernal journeys." [52]

In many archaic traditions the Cosmic Tree represented the sacredness of the world. It relates to the idea of creation, fecundity, initiation, reality, and immortality. It is one of the most universal of religious symbols and it is central to shamanism. By ascending the Cosmic Tree, the shaman gains access to the seven planetary heavens. At the seventh heaven, at the summit of the Cosmic Tree, the shaman is able to ask the future of his community and of the fate of souls.

Concepts of heaven and hell – of a God above and a Devil below – have been shattered in the popular western imagination by the advances of Science. The images of earth from space, that have been available since the 1960s, and more recently, photographs taken by the Hubble Telescope, have shaped the popular image of the universe. To talk of an "above" or a "below" when the same endless, star-studded void stretches limitlessly in all directions have left God and the Devil with nowhere to hide. The Flat Earth Society, which was still active in the 1960s, finally conceded defeat when the images of the earth from the moon appeared on our TV screens for the first time. This, of course, did not mark the death of the biblical cosmology. That had happened long ago, when Galileo turned a telescope to the heavens for the first time in history.

The tripartite division of the universe into the celestial regions, the earth, and the underworld survives as a myth that explains a deeper truth that the mere

Interpreting Shamanic Landscapes

images of a camera. It is product of the human psyche and a true expression of the regions of the soul. The three planes reflect our existential sensibilities to the vagaries of life and the products of the Unconscious. They reflect our awareness of the presence of that "Wholly Other" in the regions above, the mundane and ordinary all around us and of the demonic in human wickedness below. The ability to travel safely between the three planes is what defines the shaman.

What is interesting is to note that the shaman regarded specific places as providing the hole, or void, through which this axis passed. Such places were identified by our innate sensitivity to the sacred in certain locales. In terms of the shaman's cosmology, and that of his people, this axis might be described as a tree or a mountain, possessed of a series of levels, usually seven, or nine in number. The tree, or mountain, connects to the North Star, upon whose axis the starry skies turn. A specific tree or hill might serve to mark this axis. As a place that gave access to the gods it became a place of prayer and sacrifice. The yurt – the circular living space of the shaman – was an image of the cosmos in miniature. Within it, the central pole would serve as an image of the Cosmic Tree. The shaman might climb this pole, notched seven times to reflect the structure of the celestial regions, in order to journey into the world of the spirits and the gods.

In the middle of the sky shines the Pole Star. For many nomadic peoples, such as the Lapps and the Finns, it is the tent pole of the sky or "Pillar of the World." Thus, the tent pole of the Yurt acquires a sacred value as an earthly representation of the Sky Pillar. For the Soyot it is sacred and at its foot was placed a small stone altar. The pillar almost has the status of a god. The central pillar is a symbol for nomadic peoples the world over, including a number of Native American peoples. The pole, therefore, becomes a symbol of the shaman's ascent and descent between one cosmic zone and another:

"In the archaic cultures communicating between sky and earth is ordinarily used to send offerings to the celestial gods and not for concrete and personal ascent; the latter remains the prerogative of shamans…. The "Center of the World" is a site that permits (the community) to send their prayers and offerings to the celestial gods, whereas for (the shaman) it is a place for beginning a flight in the strictest sense of the word. Only for the latter is real communication among the three cosmic zones a possibility." [53]

Sacred places, even as they manifest themselves to modern man, have the characteristic of something that pierces both the sky and the earth. The standing stone, the sacred tree, the tower on the hill, the pyramid – all have the characteristic of joining heaven and earth and the regions below.

Interpreting Shamanic Landscapes

3.9. Cursus monuments

Cursus monuments consist of two low, continuous banks of earth, forming a linear feature across the landscape and often linking several sacred locales. They vary in length from a few hundred metres to several kilometres. Monuments such as the Dorset Cursus were clearly meant to transform the way in which a landscape is 'read', by containing and directing how it was experienced. They link monuments, which give access to the spirit realms, in a specific sequence, thus 'fixing' the shaman's journey in a form that can still be experienced five thousand years later. Cursus monuments limit and contain movement across a landscape, being designed in and of themselves for the performance of rituals. They marshal our experience and demand we see a landscape in a particular way. [54]

The Dorset Cursus consists of two parallel banks and ditches, 100 metres apart, and traverses the countryside for 10 kilometres. Richard Bradley explains how the cursus appears to be aligned on a series of significant features, more specifically, the long barrows. These may well have been the focus of the rituals that took place here. He argues that the cursus monument not only determines the flow of human experience through space but also through time:

"But at the same time, by controlling movement within such monuments, people might also have seemed to be controlling time itself. It is not that alignments of these kinds were necessary to establish a calendar. Rather, the important point is that by linking the operation of great monuments to the unchanging world of nature their builders were putting the significance of these constructions beyond any challenge. The same phenomena could be observed year after year. Through the creation of monumental architecture, society confirmed its stable structure. And it was by linking concepts of place to those of time that monuments have had such a profound influence over human experience." [55]

The containing of landscape marks a significant shift from the thinking of earlier hunter-gatherer communities. Monuments of hunter-gatherers have always been slight, marking, rather than altering natural landscapes. These early monuments might be deliberately temporary, just as we find amongst the Australian aborigines of today, who create simple sand paintings and earth sculptures in preparation for great gatherings and rituals. But monuments on the scale of those built by the pastoralists and herders of the Neolithic have begun to do more than enhance natural landscapes – they changed them forever. They begin the process that would, one day, end our holistic relationship with nature.

In his book, 'Shamanism and the Mystery Lines', Paul Devereux [56] discusses British linear monuments of the Neolithic, such as the Dorset Cursus and argues for a shamanic function. He sees a direct relationship between the creation of linear features in ritual landscapes and the spiritual landscapes of shamanic trance:

"That means there are two kinds of 'ley hunting' available to the modern alignment researcher: outer and inner. The outer involves studying ancient shamanic landscapes – on maps, air photos, and in the field. We need to look at them, find out all we can about them, learn from them. But there is an inner geography too…. There is the Spirit Earth overlying the physical lineaments of the land…." [57]

It is my own belief that linearity is of no proven significance in the mapping of shamanic landscapes. Shamanic art in the form of rock paintings illustrate journeys of complex patterning that are more to do with significant points in a landscape, rather than linear features. The San rock art studied by Lewis-Williams reveals the convoluted route of the shaman in moving through the landscape. They reflect the movements of the living, following the ancestral paths. Coastlines, highly visible natural features, rivers, mountains, forest and marsh, guide such journeys – they follow the lines of least resistance to human passage. Linearity is the child of the cartographer, not the shaman, and the sacred path between two locales is that trod by the feet of men both in the present and in the time of the ancestors.

3.10. Early Bronze Age Round Barrows.

In parts of Britain, such as Wiltshire and the chalk downlands of Dorset, parts of the Peak District and Yorkshire, Bronze Age barrows are the most numerous of our surviving prehistoric monuments. In many instances, they occupy landscapes that were made sacred in the Neolithic, indicating a continuing respect for specific sacred locales. Is there any evidence of a continuing belief in the shamanic worldview during the Bronze Age?

Certainly, lifestyles changed during the course of the twelve hundred years or so since copper and bronze tools were first used on these islands. The significant transition is not so much the advancement of metallurgy, but the growth of a sedentary lifestyle. In places like Dartmoor, we see clear evidence of the establishment of villages, the growth of arable farming – even on quite marginal land – and the wholesale destruction of Britain's forests. What is happening in Amazonia today, happened in Britain three thousand years ago. My own gut feeling is that, with the destruction of his world, the shaman was driven to the margins of society.

The major difference between a Bronze Age barrow and the megalithic tombs that preceded them is that there is no chamber as such and no access to the dead once the barrow was complete. A typical barrow contains a cist (a box made of stone

Interpreting Shamanic Landscapes

Tree covered barrow, Avebury

slabs), big enough to take the body in a foetal position, over which is built a large mound of earth or stone. Alternatively, there might be a simple cavity below the original ground surface, containing an urn of burnt bones and covered with a slab of stone. Many barrows contain grave goods, such as bronze daggers, spearheads and body ornaments, sometimes of gold. These grave goods give an insight into the status of the tomb's occupant. Some tombs in the Stonehenge complex contain what can only be described as the grave goods of kings – polished maceheads on ornate shafts, gold pectorals and magnificent lunulae of imported Irish gold. The honouring of the dead in this way differs markedly from the sparse grave goods of the Neolithic. Grave goods of this kind reflect the glorification of an individual and a growing cult of personality. The literary evidence for this can be found in the literature of the ancient Greeks, as well as our own Celtic heritage. The ancestor has ceased to be eponymous. He is honoured and remembered but he is no longer called upon to intervene in the affairs of the living. In the case of the Early Bronze Age, there is evidence that the shaman continued to hold a significant position in society and was honoured in death.

There is also evidence that the relationship between the living and the dead was becoming increasingly ambivalent. In the Neolithic, the use of ancestral bones in rituals indicates that the dead where welcomed back amongst the living. By the late Bronze Age the opposite seems to be the case. In the case of articulated burials

Interpreting Shamanic Landscapes

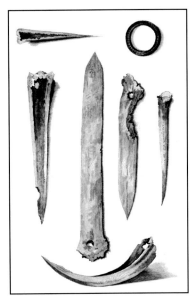

Finds from 'shaman's' grave, Upton Lovel Down. Thirty six of the pierced bones and tusks were found. (After Colt-Hoare)

(where the complete body has been interred), there is evidence for the deliberate mutilation of the dead. Ashbee describes a burial under a bowl barrow at Amesbury where the right arm was missing and the other arm disarticulated with the hand severed by a cut through the forearm. Grinsell records a case of a burial where the head had been severed prior to burial. Many burials indicate that the bodies had been trussed up prior to burial, many into a contracted foetal position. This has obvious implications for the concept of rebirth, but may also be a way of containing the dead.

Stuart Piggott produced two papers in which he advanced the evidence for shamanic practices in Bronze Age Britain, drawing from the evidence of grave goods. He produced a paper in 1962, called 'From Salisbury Plain to Siberia'. In it he re-interprets grave goods from barrow Upton Lovell G2a, which was excavated by Colt Hoare in 1801. The skeleton in Upton Lovell was accompanied by 60 bone points, which were situated near the feet and the breast of the extended skeleton, as well as stone axes. In addition there were perforated boar's tusks. He compared these finds with burials from Siberia. Stuart Piggott suggested that the bone points had formed fringes on a garment made of skins. The Siberian graves also contained stone axes. More tellingly, the Siberian graves contained T-headed drumsticks still in use amongst shamans today. He felt that the similarity between the grave assemblages and the costumes and equipment of shamans of recent times provides evidence of shamanic activity in the British Early Bronze Age. There are a number of other barrows that contained similar assemblages in Yorkshire and near Stonehenge.

Paul Ashbee also notes the possible evidence for drums. He describes evidence for the covering of the mouth of large urns, found in many barrows, with a tight cloth or skin. The overhanging rim, or crown of large cinerary urns is suited to this. He records that Colt-Hoare found an urn at Woodyates, Dorset, Barrow 17, which had eleven holes around the rim, to enable some such covering of the mouth to be secured. [58]

Such evidence as exists for the possibility of drums needs to be seen in the light of research into the acoustic effects of stone circles and their possible use for inducing shamanistic trance. This offers an ideal opportunity for some practical research by reconstructing and experimenting with such a drum. The presence of drums and shamanic apparel in Bronze Age tombs is not the only evidence for the tool-kit of the shaman. In her book 'British Barrow – A matter of life and death', Ann Woodward summarizes the argument for the survival of shamanism well into the Bronze Age:

"In fact, the ranges of equipment found in graves throughout Britain can be used to argue that the sets of ritual equipment – mainly beads of magical composi-

Interpreting Shamanic Landscapes

tion, miniature vessels, (known as incense cups, and an ideal design for burning hallucinogenic substances) and special objects selected from nature – may have belonged to specialist medicine men or shamans who practiced their important ceremonies throughout the country. The only thing that is really different about Wessex is that there is a distinct concentration of such graves around Stonehenge, near Avebury, on Cranbourne Chase, and in the Wylye valley. And that may be due to a particular historical process, whereby the practitioners of a cult which was fast becoming obsolete, or their followers, chose to bury them in the areas of their ancient ancestral monuments." [59]

Ann Woodward's comments imply that the shaman was already being linked with the cults of the past. There is further evidence for the marginalisation of the shaman on Dartmoor, where we have the surviving evidence of Bronze Age settlement patterns. In some instances, the settlements have encroached on monumental space. In the case of Merrivale, the cairns that were the focus of the entire ritual landscape had walls and huts built over them as if they no longer mattered. These settlements belong to the Late Bronze Age and early Iron Age. Of course, the odd example of the slighting of earlier monuments and the transition of tomb types does not mark the end of a belief system everywhere. I have no doubt that shamanism persisted on the margins of many communities and continued to do so well into historic times. It is his place in society that has changed. We see precisely this happening in all the communities of the world where the practice of shamanism has persisted.

Concusion

Whatever else they may be, the sacred monuments that humans add to the earth are a manifestation of our belief in the transcendent. Our shared humanity with our shaman ancestors means they can be 'read back' and interpreted with those same physical, emotional and psychic sensitivities that caused them to be built in the first place. They tap our experience of the Divine in a way that is common to all – through the innate response that Otto calls the 'numinous'. They are also ritual settings, in which the structures themselves provide a key to specific ritual movements and the beliefs they express. In our rational interpretation of ritual landscapes, as well as in our unconscious, emotional responses, these landscapes provide an unbroken link with our shaman ancestors.

In the third and final part of this book, I will be giving an account of five of Britain's most ancient ritual landscapes. In these journeys, I will develop my argument that Neolithic and Early Bronze Age ritual landscapes are essentially shamanic. In sharing these travels, I hope that you too may experience, as I have done, the shaman's dance in dust of the millennia.

Avebury, Wiltshire

Part Four

Five Shamanic Landscapes

Introduction

IN PART THREE of this book, I argued that many of Britain's prehistoric monuments reflect a belief system that is shamanic in nature. The construction of those monuments was, in turn, inspired by landscapes shaped by Nature and sanctified by the movement of the ancestors along ancient pathways. There is plenty of ethnographic evidence to support the concept that many shamans believe their power is rooted in their relationship with ancestral spirits and the energy 'stored' in specified sacred locales. The presence of the ancestors within a landscape is the source of power. Shamans sign these sacred landscapes in both simple and complex ways. At the simple level, places of power may be signed with rock carvings and rock paintings. The inspiration for these may be the trance experiences of the shaman, in the form of so-called entoptic phenomena, or encounters with ancestral and animal spirits. At the other end of the spectrum, the great passage graves of the Boyne Culture were constructed as physical gateways to the otherworld. In studying these landscapes and monuments, as archaeology and as phenomena to be experienced in an existential sense, I believe we may come close to apprehending the spirit of the shaman of our native soil.

The practice of shamanism is experiencing a western 'revival' both as a dimension of the alternative cultural scene and as a form of therapy. Carl Jung argued that the shaman of old was the original psychotherapist. Neo-shamanism in Britain appears to be constructing itself out of the practices of the shamans of Native America, Aboriginal Australia, and Latin America, to name just three sources of inspiration. These cultures may provide valuable insights into the practice of shamanism, but merely copying their practices ignores the fact that the shaman's power is rooted in familiar landscapes and the ancestral spirits it contains.

In the final section of the book, I intend to celebrate five landscapes that I believe our shaman ancestors sanctified with their sacred journeys. I will provide pointers to our shamanic past by exploring our archaeological heritage and its interplay with landscape. What you see depends on your own imagining. The journey to the otherworld goes inwards. As with the Australian Aborigines and their Dreamtime ancestors, the power of the shaman of old is seen in the interplay of the landscape's natural features and our own rich imaginations in which our mythic past is constructed.

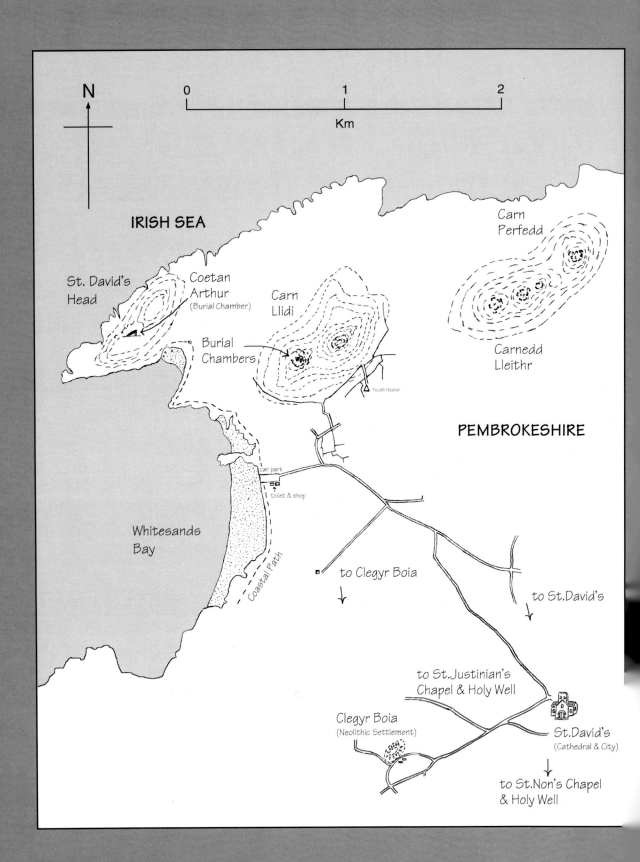

Five Shamanic Landscapes

4.1. In the Shadow of the First Stonehenge
St. David's, Pembrokeshire

In the far south west of Wales – as far west as you can go – is St. David's. The name is given both to the peninsula of land that forms the tip the southern arc of Cardigan Bay and the city itself. This tiny city – the smallest in the British Isles – has a magnificent cathedral. One wonders why such a tiny out of the way place - little more than a village really - should have attracted the wealth to build such a fine cathedral and bishop's palace and achieved such prestige throughout the Middle Ages.

The surrounding landscape conspires to share the phenomenon of miniaturization that is Saint David's. Rocky outcrops rise without warning from the plain and look much bigger than they actually are. The hills of Carn Llidi and Carn Perfedd dominate the view to the northwest. They could be distant mountains of considerable height. But it is an illusion. They are but a stroll from St. David's and may be ascended in a matter of minutes. The whole peninsula of St. David's can be walked round in a day along a coastline of sweeping cliffs, punctuated with dreamy inlets and seascapes dotted with islands. City and landscape alike are on a most human scale. And all around is the sea, dominating every perspective and diminishing still further the scale and importance of man's little achievements in this faraway place.

The shamans came here as the ice that had covered Britain for many thousands of years began its long retreat. North Wales was still in the grip of the last ice age, known as the Devensian, with glaciers carving the rugged ice-shattered mountains of what we now know as the Snowdonia National Park. On the fringes of the ice sheet, in a cold, harsh landscape not dissimilar to the Siberian steppes of the shaman of today, Stone Age man struggled to survive in the arctic tundra.

Humans occupied this part of the Pembroke coast from the early to the late Mesolithic – taking advantage of the improving climate as the ice sheets retreated, leaving a temperate and fertile environment behind. They made use of the caves along the coastline to provide shelter, as well as prominent inland sites atop rocky outcrops, that afforded both protection and a landmark to aim for when returning from the hunt.

Whitesands Bay, near St. David's, is one such place, where the hunter-gatherers of the Mesolithic left evidence of their sojourn in areas now only revealed at low tide. The sea has risen since then, and their encampments were built in the shadow of the cliffs now known as St. David's Head.

Five Shamanic Landscapes

As Britain entered the Neolithic phase and pastoralism and agriculture played an increasingly important role in providing food, the evidence from Pembroke indicates that little changed in the lifestyle of the people who lived in this remote place. Their ancient paths and stopping places became the locations for semi-permanent settlements but the evidence points to a culture subsisting largely by hunting and gathering, with some herding of cattle.

What is so special about St. David's?

As with all ancient landscapes, its power is generated by energies that have been sedimented in the landscape through the spiritual acts of a thousand generations. Once the shaman has planted the Cosmic Tree, holy men are drawn to the spot thereafter - for here is the tear in the veil through which the gods come to earth. Christians now worship where Celts once made offerings to the spirits of the woods, streams, and sacred springs. The Celts worshipped in groves where the shaman of the Bronze Age and the Neolithic had climbed his Cosmic Tree and entered the trance state that took him to the gods. They in turn, obsessed with the sanctity of the ancestors, had built their huts where their Mesolithic forbears left evidence of their camps in the period following the retreat of the last Ice Age. It is difficult to eradicate sanctity. Time simply modifies the architecture and changes the names of the gods. Churches and place-names around St. David's celebrate saints that are merely the old Celtic deities hiding behind a thin, Christian veneer. The holy wells of St. David's were undoubtedly holy wells long before the Christians came. The unusual siting of the great cathedral itself may well mark the location of a druid grove in a place where Druidism long outlasted the Roman onslaught.

The Neolithic tomb monuments in this part of Pembrokeshire - some fifty in number - attest to its importance all those years ago. Guided by the great crowns of ice-shattered rock that crown the Preseli mountains, traders and adventurers from Ireland and the Mediterranean used the many harbours dotted about this headland to bring their goods to land. Porth y Rhaw, St. Non's Bay, Porth Clais, Porth Stinian and Whitesand Bay all provide safe harbour and are less than an hour on foot for the trader and his goods from St. David's. Here landed traders of the Bronze Age, bearing Irish gold, on their way to do business with the wealthy farmers of Wessex. Gold lunulae, of Irish provenance, have been found in Bronze Age barrows built within the great Stonehenge barrow cemetery and undoubtedly passed this way on their journey to that great sanctuary in the East.

By Celtic Christian times the little landing places used by the Neolithic and Bronze Age traders had small chapels, such as the chapel of St. Non and St. Justinian. The ruins of these early chapels survive to this day, and, in the case of St. Non's, is still tended by nuns living in the retreat house close by. The great

Five Shamanic Landscapes

hero saints of the Celtic Christian period – St. Patrick, St. David, St. Bridget and many others, undoubtedly sanctified the earth on which we walk, drawing their spiritual sustenance from the energy left in the earth by the Shaman and the Druid who walked these paths before them.

A short stroll from St. David's is a rocky outcrop known as Clegyr Boia. Here we find a rare and important example of a Neolithic settlement, with the remains of fortifications that many now accept belong to the same period. Looking to the northwest and St. David's Head, the skyline is dominated by Carn Llidi and Carn Perfedd, where the inhabitants of Clegyr Boia built three tombs. Their tombs are small, reflecting the available manpower of these tiny communities and their relatively poor lifestyle, based mainly on fishing and hunting. From Clegyr Boia the Stone Age herdsmen could watch the sun setting over the paths linking headlands and rocky outcrops, where the tombs of the ancestors are hidden by the growing shadows. Here, for sure, the Shaman danced and called upon the spirits to heal the ills of his people.

Most significant of all for Pembrokeshire is the link between this isolated land and Stonehenge. It was in 1923 that H.H. Thomas identified the 'bluestones' of Stonehenge as dolerite coming from a restricted outcrop between Carnmenyn and Foel Trigarn in the Preseli Hills. How the stones travelled from the Preseli to Stonehenge – a distance of over 130 miles – remains the mystery

Pentre Ifan Dolmen, Pembrokeshire, with Carn Ingli in the background, source of the Stonehenge Bluestones

Shamanism and Sacred Landscapes

Five Shamanic Landscapes

and a cause of much controversy in archaeological and geological circles. Some have argued that they were brought to Salisbury Plain by glacial action – although there is no evidence for glacial flows in anything like the right direction. Others argue that they were ferried around the coastal bays of the south west coast of Britain and up the River Avon to within a few miles of Stonehenge. A team of schoolboys managed the feat of ferrying a concrete replica up the River Avon in the 1960s, demonstrating the technical feasibility for a Neolithic culture.

Aubrey Burl is a strong advocate of the glacial erratic theory – but his main argument is simply that all stone circles are built with the nearest available stone. Rodney Castleden points out that there is little geological evidence to support the glacial erratic theory, despite a watching brief since the 1970s to uncover such evidence. Even the cutting of the route of the M5, right across the path of all the potential approaches for glacial moraine and outwash, revealed nothing to support the glacial theory. We are left, therefore, with the fact that, at the time of Stonehenge, the Preseli was a land so sacred that it was worth carrying great stones that huge distance in order to connect these two sacred landscapes. For me, the issue is simple. The fact that the builders of Stonehenge acquired so many stones from the Preseli of suitable size effectively rules out the gathering of the odd glacial erratic. [1]

In June 2004, evidence emerged which finally seemed to tie the Stonehenge bluestones to the Preseli. The graves of what appears to be a late Neolithic family of seven were uncovered at Boscombe Down, close to Stonehenge, during road improvement work. They have been referred to as the 'Boscombe Bowmen' because of the presence of flint arrowheads in the grave. The great discovery came with the chemical analysis of their teeth. The water we drink as children leaves an identifiable chemical trace in the enamel of our teeth and this can be used to identify where a person spent their childhood. The remarkable discovery is that these men appear to have grown up close to the Preseli Mountains, thus providing a powerful link between Stonehenge and this part of Wales. Might we think in terms of a group of people, migrating to the richer ground of Wessex, deciding to take their sacred earth with them – in the form of stones from their holy mountain [2]

My own belief, although I admit no evidence to prove it, is that the bluestones may well have been a pre-existing stone circle in the Preseli and the entire structure was excavated and moved east to become the first stones of Stonehenge.

In his book 'Shamanism and the Mystery Lines', Paul Devereux describes how he visited the blue dolerite outcrops of Carn Ingli in the Preseli Mountains, as part of his Dragon Project of 1986. Devereux discusses the powerful magnetic content of the rocks and their potential impact on the temporal lobes of the

Five Shamanic Landscapes

brain. This, he says, may have influenced the visions of St. Brynach, a sixth century Celtic anchorite who dwelt in these hills. This has obvious implications for their use by the shamans of the Neolithic. Many other writers have discussed the potential influence of the electro-magnetic properties of certain types of stone on human perception. Modern shamans still make considerable use of stones, particularly quartzite, in their rituals. [3]

I was drawn to the Preseli and St. David's in the early nineties, having read a book by Gaynor Francis, called 'The First Stonehenge'[4], which discussed the intervisibility of peaks in the Preseli and their alignment with heavenly bodies. The book argued for a sacredness of place that went back to the last years of the Ice Age. At Preseli, Ms. Francis argues, our Mesolithic ancestors developed a knowledge of celestial bodies and their risings, based on alignments between the different summits of the Preseli hills. This knowledge was eventually translated, along with the sacred stones of the Preseli, to the plains of Wessex and the complex celestial alignments of the Stonehenge stones themselves

Choosing a path in this beautiful and unspoilt country is not easy. Gaynor Francis offered routes that explore the complex alignments that she claims for the Preseli, but some of these can be rather isolated and forbidding, particularly when there is low cloud and mist. The tombs of the Ancestors are scattered all along this coastline and a great week – or fortnight – can be had by acquiring a gazetteer and visiting as many as you can to make your own offerings to the dead.

I chose, rather, to seek the shaman in the lands where he left the clearest evidence for his occupation and undoubtedly sought his living. I started my shamanic quest in St. David's itself, in the belief that sanctity draws sanctity and this is the sacred heart of this strange and beautiful landscape. From St. David's it is a pleasant, level stroll to the Pembrokeshire coast, which many regard as the most beautiful in the British Isles. Why our ancestors should choose to build their Houses of Eternity along this magnificent coast is plain for all to see.

The landscape of St. David's has changed a great deal since the Mesolithic. Glaciers that once covered Wales continued to retreat, raising sea levels and causing some stretches of land to rise and others to fall as the weight of ice melted into the sea. The savage environment of their Paleolithic ancestors, with its arctic tundra populated with woolly mammoth, rhinoceros, bears and bison was fast becoming the temperate climate we know today.

We have found the stopping places of the hunter-gatherers of the Mesolithic fashioned their tools, made beads and even a small Venus figurine. But much is lost. Beneath the sea lie the forests where they hunted. The islands that are scattered about the coast were, until nine or ten thousand years ago, set within a lowland landscape of forest and marsh.

Five Shamanic Landscapes

Thousands of years later, the descendents of these post-glacial inhabitants would build their tombs close by the places made sacred by their ancestors. We can be sure that each path was named and each cliff and rocky eminence had legends attached that had been passed down through oral tradition. As Christopher Tilley points out:

"These, no doubt named, natural topographic features would have been invested with sets of local meanings and would have had the effect of pinpointing the position of camp sites...clearly deciding to stop at a particular place was much more than simply a matter of food acquisition." [5]

When the Stonehenge and Avebury cultures were moving toward creating great surpluses of agricultural wealth and using them to build their astonishing monuments, things changed little here. The evidence is that hunting and gathering and limited pastoralism remained the lifestyle throughout the Neolithic. When the high priest or the king led the ceremonies at the spectacular monuments of Avebury and Stonehenge, the local shaman remained the important religious figure in these quieter parts. They would have watched as the traders from the West brought Irish gold to these coasts – not for them – but for their wealthy neighbours, who lived on the chalk downlands to the East. And they would have watched as the men from the East came to take their sacred bluestones away, to build their temple on Salisbury Plain.

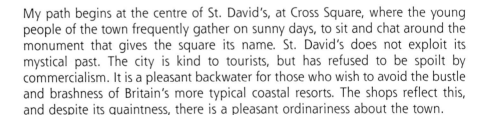

My path begins at the centre of St. David's, at Cross Square, where the young people of the town frequently gather on sunny days, to sit and chat around the monument that gives the square its name. St. David's does not exploit its mystical past. The city is kind to tourists, but has refused to be spoilt by commercialism. It is a pleasant backwater for those who wish to avoid the bustle and brashness of Britain's more typical coastal resorts. The shops reflect this, and despite its quaintness, there is a pleasant ordinariness about the town.

The magnificent Cathedral of St. David's and the ruins of the Bishop's Palace, where plays and concerts are performed in the summer, are built in a hollow below Cross Square. Its sunken position required the building of a bell tower on the high ground above, so that the faithful would hear the call to worship in the town and beyond. I cannot think of any other cathedral that seems to have been located to be as inconspicuous as possible. For sure, this particular locale meant something to the Cathedral builders. The cathedral shares the narrow valley in which it is built with the River Alun and the ruins of the Bishop's Palace. It is an idyllic location, but it looks as if the weight of the cathedral has made the ground sink like a collapsed Yorkshire Pudding, so odd it is to see a magnificent cathedral built on ground so much lower than the town itself.

Five Shamanic Landscapes

Inside the church one can see that the damp ground has yielded to the weight of the great Norman pile and all the pillars of the nave now splay outwards. St. David preached a raw Celtic Christianity here, supplanting the old gods of this place. A beautiful wooded dell surrounds it today and I am sure druids came here to worship their gods of wood and stream.

Walking from the busy Cross Square I pass the stern-looking Tabernacle Church, whose Presbyterian starkness is so typical of Welsh chapels. At the walls of the ruined Bishop's Palace I pause to admire the magnificent view of the Cathedral, before leaving the city for the country lanes beyond.

The road to the coast offers the choice of Treginnis or St. Justinian. At St. Justinian there is an ancient chapel and a well – a reminder of its Celtic Christian past. The road to Treginnis leads to Clegyr Boia, and the ghost of the Stone Age settlement that once stood there. The land undulates gently, but is punctuated by a scatter of rocky outcrops that form very distinctive landmarks. Clegyr Boia is one such outcrop, rising about thirty-five metres above the average height of the surrounding landscape and is clearly visible once one has left St. David's.

To the untrained eye there is little to see at Clegyr Boia. It is possible to make out the walls that defended this Stone Age settlement, although they are now covered with a mixed growth of heather, gorse, grass and ferns. The views are magnificent, with the rocky summits of Carn Llidi and Carn Perfedd dominating the skyline to the northwest. Looking back toward St. David's, the extra height gives an excellent view of the Cathedral and the line of the beautiful vale in which it is built.

It is difficult to appreciate how important this place is, when there is so little to see on the ground. The site was excavated in 1902 and in more detail in 1953. The excavations revealed a small Neolithic settlement. Evidence of Neolithic occupation sites is very rare in Britain and here was found the remains of three Neolithic huts and a midden. Some argument remains as to the age of the defensive stone wall and it has been suggested that the surviving wall may belong to the Celtic period. The southern hut was a rectangular structure, 7 metres by 3, whilst a hut to the northern edge of the platform was more oval in shape. The southern hut, built into an angle of the outcropping rock, had two rows of four postholes and stone footings on one of the long sides.[6] Pottery was found dating to the middle Neolithic and the bones of cattle. Limpet shells were found in the midden and the charcoal of hazel, oak and birch. The plan of the third hut is less certain, as this was excavated in the nineteenth century and poorly recorded.[7]

For me, the significance of Clegyr Boia lies not only in the evidence of the dwellings of our Neolithic forbears, but also in the visual alignments with the realms of the Ancestors. Looking to the northwest, I can see Carn Llidi and St.

Five Shamanic Landscapes

David's Head, where three tombs of the Neolithic period are located. Although the tombs themselves cannot be seen, their exact location can be worked out because they were built close to distinctive rocky outcrops. It is a marvellous symbolism. From the land of the living we may look to the realms of the dead, illuminated from where we stand by the light of the setting sun.

Between the two is largely flat terrain. The path of the shaman between the two worlds could not be clearer. We may stand on the same spot where he built his hearth and watch his dance by the dusk light, as the wind whips the fire sparks into the night sky. When he journeys we may follow the setting sun to where he has gone.

View of Carn Llidi and Whitesands Bay from the coastal path

The preparation of the dead in Neolithic times commonly involved excarnation – waiting for the flesh to rot from the bones, even allowing the flesh to be consumed by carrion birds – prior to final burial. The remaining bones would then be gathered up and placed in a communal tomb. The gathered bones would represent the power of the eponymous Ancestors, with whom the shaman would commune on behalf of the living. It is not to stretch our imagination too far to imagine the rocky platforms above the tombs being used to expose the corpses of this small community prior to burial. It may have been a part of the shaman's role to assist in the translation of bones, inasmuch as it is the shaman's role in many communities to assist in the movement of the dead from this world to the next.

From Clegyr Boia a quiet road leads to a gravel track and on to Whitesands Bay. The OS map shows a lake to the left, called Pwll Trefeiddan. This shallow lake,

Five Shamanic Landscapes

overgrown with reeds, is fed by a number of springs that make their appearance in wet weather. It is so overgrown with reeds that under normal circumstances no water is visible from the road. It serves as a reminder of the nature of this landscape before it was tamed by millennia of farmers. Marsh and forest characterized this low-lying land with the coastal paths, linking the settlements and tombs as the safest routes through this almost primordial world. Now easy paths and tracks take me to Whitesands Bay and the tombs of Carn Llidi and St. David's Head. The Pembrokeshire coast is arguably the finest coastal walk in Britain, not least because it facilitates visits to many ancient tombs, as well as the pretty coastal villages of more recent times. I join the Coast Path as it follows a low shelving cliff that runs along the back of the beach.

Whitesands Bay was populated during the Mesolithic, long before the Neolithic settlements at Clegyr Boia. Many Mesolithic settlements have been discovered around the southern Pembrokeshire coast, indicating that this area was extensively exploited. Sea levels were lower then and the present coast was further inland. The rising sea (a result of post-glacial global warming) has drowned the hunting grounds of the first people to reoccupy this land after the retreat of the ice. The land itself has also risen as a result of the relief from the overlying weight of glacial ice. In the post-glacial period dense woodland and marsh occupied what is now the bay. Woodland of oak, hazel and alder and stretches of marsh joined Ramsey Island to the mainland. It is only at low tide that evidence emerges of the first post-glacial settlements in the form of scatters of flint from the manufacture of flint tools. Indeed, the evidence for settlement in the Mesolithic in Pembrokeshire – the Time of the Shaman - is entirely coastal.

Sadly, what is left to us – fishing implements, scatters of flint where they made their fine microlith tools and shell middens – tell us very little about their religious beliefs and practices. In the Pembrokeshire area, at Nab Head a shale 'Venus' figurine was found and a large quantity of perforated shale beads. We know that they traded such things but can discover little else. We also know that the use of some habitation sites continued for thousands of years, despite the rapidly changing landscape as the seas encroached.

We may assume that the first communities to occupy this land following the retreat of the last Ice Age had a powerful affinity with place. The strange rocky outcrops that dominate this landscape would have been special to them, just as unusual natural features are special to Australian Aborigines and many other indigenous peoples today. These were their paths and dancing grounds, as they followed a pattern of seasonal migration that had evolved through the traditions of a thousand years. As Christopher Tilley suggests of this type of landscape:

Five Shamanic Landscapes

"It was precisely because the coast provided both rich economic resources and a wealth of named and distinctive natural topographic markers that it was so symbolically important to both Mesolithic and Neolithic populations. During the Mesolithic it seems highly likely that settlement locales represent places on paths of movement, bound into the lie of the land at marked changes of relief with a cosmological significance, which were ordered sequentially in relation to each other." [8]

Nothing remains at Whitesands Bay to be seen by the casual eye. On hot summer days, sun worshippers bask on its unspoilt beaches, unaware, one suspects, of the traces of human habitation that go back to the time when the glaciers retreated from where they now lie.

Coetan Arthur Dolmen, St. David's Head

The walk along Whitesands Bay north to St. David's Head is about two kilometres, before one arrives at a car park and slipway and a shop that sells ice cream and soft drinks in high season. A gate on the far side of the car park gives access to the continuation of the path toward St. David's Head.

A sign on the gate bears the legend "Site of St. Patrick's Chapel – Scheduled Ancient Monument'. This serves as another reminder of the sanctity of this place. Sadly, modern maps show no sign of the chapel and there is nothing to be seen above ground. But the attraction lies ahead – and the attachment of the name of Arthur to one of the three burial chambers built on this peninsula is a pull for even the less informed tourist. They seek Coetan Arthur, the magnificent burial chamber at St. David's Head. The tourists I come across here are from all over the world – Germans, Americans, Japanese, Dutch and so on. It seems a long way to come to visit such an out of

Five Shamanic Landscapes

the way place – until you remember that it is also en route via, the ferry from Fishguard, to that other Celtic paradise – Eire. Indeed, they are doing no more than continuing a tradition that goes back six thousand years, to the time when the traders of the Neolithic and the Bronze Age plied the waters of the Irish Sea with their polished flint axe heads, burnished pottery and fine Irish gold.

Scanning the crest of St. David's Head from the path above Porthmelgan, it is possible to make out Coetan Arthur in a gap in the line of an outcrop of rocks. This gap in the rocks focuses our attention on the great capstone, which lies propped against its single, surviving orthostat. The line of rocks forms a natural amphitheatre for the tomb. The positioning is deliberate. It occupies the most prominent spot on this headland, in virtually the only location where it could be seen at a distance.

An anonymous description of the tomb, written in 1864, gives us as accurate a description of Coetan Arthur as can be provided:

"The excursionists' attention was next directed to the mutilated remains of a cromlech, or sepulchral chamber...a very fair specimen, of moderate dimensions. The structure at present consists of the remains of its supporters (once probably six in number) and a covering stone. A huge mass of rock lies touching part of it, which looks as if it had at one time formed a portion of the gallery or chamber. There are also the remains of original small, dry masonry, by which the gaps between the larger stones were always carefully filled up. Few traces of its former covering, or tumulus, could be made out." [9]

Some believe Coetan Arthur to be the remains of a passage tomb, linking it with the common traditions of the Atlantic seaboard from as far apart as Spain and Ireland. The evidence for this is thin, however, and its original appearance remains a mystery. It may have had a cairn, or its great triangular capstone may have remained visible, with drystone walling filling the voids between the supporting orthostats. We must guess at its original architecture, and indeed, the contents of the tomb, for none have been found. The acid soil of this area has a tendency to rot bones, leaving little for the archaeologist. The tomb was excavated in 1898, but no finds were recorded.[10] We must permit our imaginations, rather, to build the tomb anew and see the closed entrance to the tomb by the light of a flickering fire in the gathering darkness. The shaman is here to dance and drum so that he may walk through the closing stone and enter the Land of the Ancestors. We do not know the mythologies of the peoples of the British Neolithic, for they did not write or leave pictorial representations that we can interpret. But their most impressive monuments were their tombs. These often had – as is the case with Pentre Ifan in the Preseli - a ceremonial courtyard before the entrance to the tomb. Surrounded by an arc of megaliths, they provided a

Five Shamanic Landscapes

setting for sacred theatre whose focus was the gateway to the otherworld. The liminal character of these tomb courtyards is transparent. Built in places of great significance, that were a gateway into the West, with the sealed portal serving the same purpose as the Cosmic Tree of shamanic mythology. They are the nexus with the spirit world – the embarkation point for the shaman in his ritual flight to do business with the dead. Today it is possible, if you can sit without trembling beneath the weight of the barely supported capstone, to experience the spirit realms.

And from this magnificent spot, where we may gaze across the Irish Sea to the West and the setting sun, the meaning could not be more transparent. Here, like life, the land comes to an end. At the close of the day, we witness the death of the sun. We know where the dead have gone. I follow the setting sun in the ship of my imagination to the otherworld, where it lights the land of my ancestors.

I turn back and walk the way I have come. On the other side of the valley, is Carn Llidi, the sacred mountain that brought me here. A well-made track winds around the base of the hill. To either side is thick gorse and fern so I cannot lose my way. It is a longer route than heading straight up to the summit, but the tombs I seek lie just off the track and sticking to it will make their location easier. I am looking for a cracked, concrete platform and a pair of iron gateposts, the remnants of a long demolished building. Close by, almost hugging the face of the rock, are two, tiny tombs, barely four foot square in their interior space.

At a glance, these overgrown remains are easy to mistake for natural features. Closer examination reveals their purposeful structure and the magnificence of their location. One of the capstones has fallen from its surviving orthostats and leans crookedly, draped in ivy. The second is more complete, and it is possible to crawl into the tiny space beneath the capstone and enter the space where the dead sleep. Nothing remains of any cairn that may have covered these tombs, and there are no records of finds. If once covered with a cairn, these tombs probably formed a single entity with two chambers.

Whatever the truth of the matter, the tombs were not built to draw the eye. Rather, they share in the monumentality of Carn Llidi, to which the living might turn, from many miles away, and fly to those who have gone into the West.

To approach this Mountain of the Dead, once night had fallen, must have brought fear and trembling to those who came to make offerings of meat and milk. The path I have ascended may have been the ancient path from Clegyr Boia. The summit platform of Carn Llidi, not these hidden tombs, would have

Five Shamanic Landscapes

been the place of the shaman's dance. This summit is the highest point for miles, almost six hundred feet above the sea below and surely would have been the shaman's gateway to the stars. This is the Cosmic Mountain of old, linking all the worlds and sanctified by the presence of the dead.

I leave the mountain by the way I came, following the path back to the world of the living. At the switchback junction in the path, I continue to circle the mountain away from St. David's Head and toward the track that will take me to the Youth Hostel. From the hostel it is a pleasant, reflective walk along quiet tracks to the road that links Whitesands Bay with St. David's. Two kilometres along this road, which sees little traffic – being a road to nowhere but a beach – brings me back to St. David's and the start of my walk.

Small tomb, Carn Llidi, St. David's

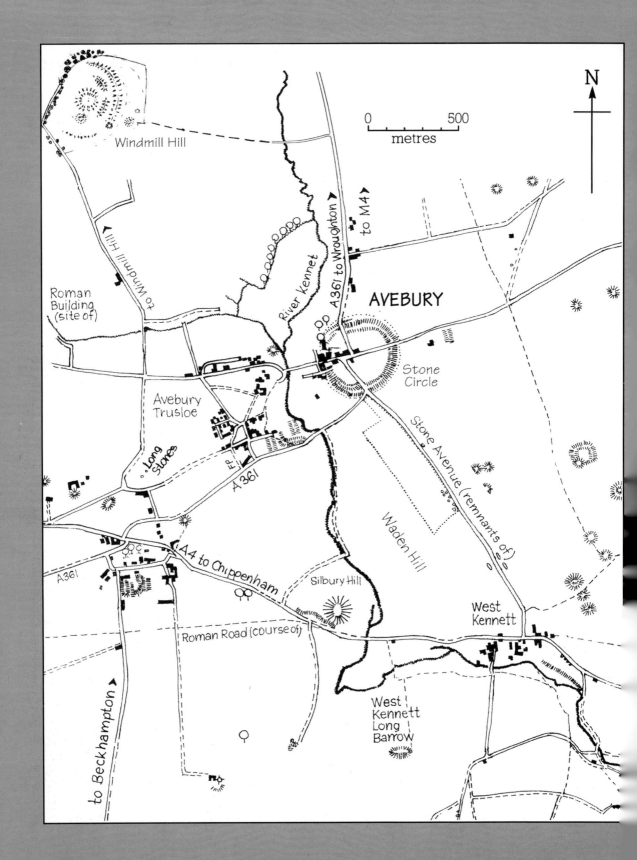

Five Shamanic Landscapes

4.2. Shamans of a Lost Kingdom
Avebury

Think first on this at Avebury. Think of the ridiculous, impossible task of dragging a vast misshapen lump of rock for several miles and then setting it upright – all fifty tons of it - with the same delicacy as balancing a coin on its edge. Think of the man who strained on the ropes with hundreds of others to haul the megalith upright. Think of him and the sons that followed, who raised six hundred such megaliths. His sweat and blood, his unquestioning belief, gives more meaning to these stones than the musings of a hundred scholars. Think of him with humility. His work will endure when you and I, and the dusty books are all forgot.

Part of the main circle at Avebury

Since his time two hundred generations have come and gone. Some came to worship amongst the stones, acknowledging the presence of the old gods and the spirits of the long dead. The Saxons found other uses for Avebury, utilizing its great ditch and bank as a fortress during the time of Arthur. Others came to destroy. Christian fanatics and greedy landowners have torn down many stones. In the 1930s Alexander Keiller bought the monument and halted the destruction. Avebury is his gift to the future.

Tourists come to Avebury in thousands, attracted by the ill-defined mystique that attaches itself to stone circles. We come with arrogance and humility, with questions and theories, or simply to entertain the kids with tales of druidry and witchcraft. William Stukeley came in the 1720s and falsified his measurements of the stones to create serpents and Druids where there were none. Others have searched for, and found, goddesses galore, gaping vulvas and all.

Shamanism and Sacred Landscapes

Five Shamanic Landscapes

Part of the main circle at Avebury

Theories concerning mystical alignments and megalithic yards have all been teased out of the stones and proclaimed to the world as it they were writ on the earth itself.

They are not.

The dream of the shaman shaped this sacred place. It is the cosmos of his soul that stretches before you. Now he lies beneath your feet. Earth fills the mouth of the man who sang of the eagle that sits on the ninth branch of the Tree of Heaven. Talk to him. He will tell you what the stones are for.

The shaman speaks to me as I lie on the warm grass, inches from the space where his thoughts grew. I don't need crystals or dowsing rods to divine him. He shares my body for a little while as he cuts the throat of the proud-antlered deer that will carry him into the iron soul of the sky. Its blood warms me, pouring from the sun on this clear blue day as he dizzies his people with his flight to the gods. I have loved him like no other. I too, one day, will be stripped of flesh. I will lie where his bones once rested above

Five Shamanic Landscapes

the earth and the ravens fought for his eyes. I will join him where the western horizon meets the sky.

Like love, we have a relationship with the land that insinuates itself into our guts. The land has a spirit, which is present in the green fields, the rocks and stones, in running water and the wind in the trees. The people who built Avebury experienced the same soul and manifested their experience collectively in the building of a great monument. By walking the land I can draw on their power. Avebury will build itself anew in the landscapes of my soul.

1½ miles from Avebury is a holy place known as the Sanctuary. A timber building once stood here. It was so sacred they built an avenue of standing stones to link it with the great circle at Avebury. Another avenue, of which but one stone survives, links Avebury to a long barrow and a stone cove at Beckhampton, a mile to the west. These were places that could not be ignored in the new disposition. Sanctity, not practicality designed Avebury and the immovability of sacred locales is here expressed in stone. And what of Silbury Hill, which, far from seeking grandeur, is concealed in a valley bottom? Was the mythical King Sil constrained by the divination of the shaman to build where the spirits of stream and spring had sanctified the earth?

A thousand years before the first stone was raised at Avebury a huge camp, surrounded by three deep ditches and banks was built on a hill a mile to the northwest. It is now known as 'Windmill Hill causewayed enclosure'. Windmill Hill was Britain's first great monument, built by a people, who in this containment of space proclaimed a new age. They had burned forests and furrowed the scorched earth to grow wheat and barley and to create grazing for their cattle. In so doing they had forged a new alliance with nature and begun a process that would multiply the peoples of the earth a thousandfold. Windmill Hill lies close to the Ridgeway, the oldest surviving road in Europe, and the traders of cattle and fine polished axes undoubtedly used the road to reach the great camp. A hundred generations came here from the marshlands and moors to the west, from the mountains of Wales or the rugged axe quarries in the far north to barter, feast and honour the dead. Some practiced transhumance, following the herds of deer through an annual round of grazing places, culminating with the fair at Windmill Hill, where they traded skins, antler picks and dried venison for pottery or polished stone axes. We know from the evidence of such peoples from around the globe, that shamanism would have been central to their spirituality, bringing success to the hunt, curing sickness, and defeating evil spirits.

At Windmill Hill I recently found a fragment of pottery, brought to the surface by moles. The sherd was identified as Neolithic 'Grooved Ware' – common

Five Shamanic Landscapes

enough in the pits and ditches of this ancient monument. This fragment is the truth in the earth, and I may be sure of a manufacture, a use, and a disposal of something made five thousand years ago. I know there was a hand that grubbed up the clay from the riverbank and mixed it with grit. I know that fingers shaped the curved rib that decorates the pot. In the cool of the evening a fire blazed and at its heart the work was completed. All this was long ago. I have a broken, weathered fragment of a small clay vessel, which connects me directly, intimately, with the soul who made it. Perhaps it was the shaman's hand that broke it, scattering the fragments across the world to the horizons of the dead.

Archaeologists can now tell me a great deal more about my sherd of fired clay. Examination of the grits will tell me where it was made. Some pottery from Windmill Hill came from Cornwall, in the days of trackless wastes and endless forest. Further investigation can trace organic molecules in the clay. These tell what kind of food or drink the vessel carried. This means more to me than musings about lines of energy and pregnant goddesses. This is the truth about the folk who built Avebury long ago.

Silbury Hill, from the river Kennet, west of Avebury

Alexander Keiller excavated part of Windmill Hill in the 1930s. He thought it one of the most beautiful places on earth, with its uninterrupted views to the far horizons of his beloved Wiltshire. He found substantial amounts of ancient refuse, spanning the entire period of the camp's long existence as a Neolithic and Bronze Age ritual centre. The sherds of over 1300 broken pots and countless cattle bones provide evidence that people came to Windmill Hill to trade, feast and carry out ritual acts. Phallic objects, such as chalk penises and balls have been found at Windmill Hill, no doubt part of an assemblage of cult objects that have not survived or are yet to be discovered. Also found in the ditches were human remains. Evidence suggests that the bones may have

Five Shamanic Landscapes

been carried from the long barrow at West Kennet for use in rituals we can only guess at.[11] Keiller found pottery and flint implements from all over Britain. There is pottery from the Lizard peninsula in Cornwall, from the Cotswolds and from Frome, in Somerset. There are remains of stone axes from Cornwall, the Langdales in Cumbria and the Prescelly Mountains in South Wales. Windmill Hill is the beginning of Avebury's story. It is right that a journey through this sacred landscape should make Windmill Hill its first destination.[12]

My walk to Windmill Hill begins at Avebury Post Office, which stands just inside the great circle, along with the Red Lion Inn and a clutter of fine old houses. Turning left I walk past the great ditch and bank of the Avebury henge, and along the main village street toward Avebury Manor. To the right, just before the churchyard a grandiose Georgian gateway catches the eye. This is the main entrance to the manor, and reflects, as does the house itself, our insatiable desire to confer a little petty grandeur on our brief lives. But the churchyard reminds us that, however high we build and however mighty we conceive ourselves to be, only a few decades separates the healthiest of us from the dust. Good Victorian talk this, as suits the atmosphere that settles dreamily on our shoulders as we leave the tourists and the noisy traffic behind and gaze at the sightless windows and the fleeting spirits of the dead.

This is a pretty village, with an eclectic mix of architectural styles and materials used in its construction. There are old clay tiles, rustic brick and ancient sarsens, Georgian grandeur and simple thatched cottages with tiny windows. Lucky the people who live behind the chintz curtains and delicate lace. You are still amongst the stones. Many of Avebury's great megaliths were broken up to build the walls and cottages of the village. Thankfully, the ravages have stopped and this World Heritage Site is unlikely to change much for the foreseeable future. The ownership of most of the village by the National Trust ensures that the ravages of commercialisation are kept to a couple of shops and two fine museums in ancient buildings.[13]

I take a narrow lane that curves sharp right, past more cottages of thatch and ancient tile, and follow it as it passes the grounds of the manor house, sadly concealed behind a high wooden fence. The lane shrinks to a path and just before the path crosses the River Kennett I took my ease on a wooden bench, a relic of the Millennium celebrations, which provides an excellent photo opportunity of Silbury Hill. Shortly after the bench, there is a small stone bridge over the River Kennett. Here the path divides and I followed the right hand fork, with its accompanying winterbourne. The northern skyline is dominated by the long, low eminence of Windmill Hill. A large Bronze Age barrow on the crest of the hill is clearly visible. After the open space we come to Benning's Yard, with its black-painted clapboard barn. Opposite, a traditional thatch-topped wall is constructed out of sarsen blocks. Possibly, some of these stones were

Five Shamanic Landscapes

once part of the shattered monoliths that lined the processional way to Beckhampton Long Barrow.

At the end of the lane of thatched and tiled cottages, there is a shallow pond on the left and a cottage called Swan House on the right. Here I take a diversion from the route marked on the standard tourist guide and follow the hedged bridleway between the houses and toward the open fields. The bridleway crosses a little stream and then there is a metal gate, which gives access to a path, heading west to Horslip Bridge. Appropriately for a shamanic journey, this path follows a stream. Streams, rivers, hills and natural eminences of one kind our another are the shaman's guide through any landscape. They are both natural lines of energy and a source of life. In chalk country particularly, water is a precious thing, scarce on the higher ground. The villages in this area are built alongside streams and springs, and in some instances are built on land that has been settled since the Bronze Age. It was in the meadows and floodplains and the forest glades that cattle would have grazed and begun the process of enriching the earth for the crops that would follow. At Horslip Bridge I leave the fields to rejoin the metalled lane. The lane is a creamy chalky colour, with its layer of dried chalk mud carried from the fields and lanes by farm vehicles. It gives it a pleasing natural appearance and when tarmac gives way to natural chalk further up the lane you barely notice the difference. There is a fine, open feeling to the road, vehicles are rare and it enables you to think your way back as we follow a path that is probably as old as Avebury itself.

It is a ten minute stroll from Horslip Bridge to Windmill Hill. A gate and National Trust sign guide you in. It takes an informed eye to see the treasures in the earth. Mostly I have the place to myself, but the occasional walker will pause and simply not see what there is to look at. The guide books promise an excellent view of Avebury and its stones and I have experienced more than one sigh of disappointment as I point out to walkers that Avebury is almost entirely concealed by the trees that shelter the village.

Windmill Hill is popular with the locals for exercising dog and horse alike. Hardly any day-trippers come here and yet its archaeological significance is as great as Avebury. Why so little interest today? The unique profile of Windmill Hill causewayed enclosure is only apparent from the air. A few arcs of silted up ditches and the remnants of some low-lying banks are all that remains. There are three concentric circles of ditches and banks in all, now so worn down they are only prominent in the south-eastern quadrant. More prominent are the Bronze Age barrows, built in the enclosure's shadow years, when the culture that built it was long dead. There are several fine barrows scattered across the twenty acre monument.

And yet, as causewayed enclosures go, this is one of the best preserved in the country, matched only by Knap Hill, a few miles to the south of Avebury. The

Five Shamanic Landscapes

majority of surviving causewayed enclosures show little or nothing on the ground, apparent only as crop marks in times of drought or as the gentlest of undulations on the ground. It was only in the 1920s with the advent of aerial photography of ancient monuments that causewayed enclosures began to be more fully appreciated. So significant is Windmill Hill it gave its name to the entire culture identified as the early Neolithic.[14]

William Stukeley visited the camp in 1719, describing it as a 'pretty round apex, the turf as soft as velvet. There is the sign of a very old camp cast up one half of it but unfinished.'. It is not so much unfinished as worn away by natural weathering and the plough. There were always gaps in the ditches and banks, which archaeologists refer to as 'causeways', and Stukeley may have mistaken these for an unfinished work. The ground surface itself naturally weathers on chalk downs and the plough has done much to finish off what remains of our early Neolithic heritage. Richard Jefferies, writing in the 1870s, records one such act of destruction:

"Above, on the summit, is another ancient camp, and below two more turf-grown tumuli, low, and shaped like an inverted bowl. Many more have been ploughed down, doubtless in the course of the years: sometimes still as the ploughshare travels through the soil there is a sudden jerk, and a scraping sound of iron against stone, to find a jar, as he thinks – in fact a funeral urn. Like all uneducated people, in the Far East as well as in the West, he is imbued with the idea of finding hidden treasure, and breaks the urn in pieces to discover – nothing; it is empty. He will carry the fragments home to the farm, where, after a moment's curiosity, they will be thrown away with potsherds and finally used to mend the floor of a cowpen." [15]

In view of more recent finds at Avebury, where the grave of a Bronze Age bowman has revealed a wealth as great as the Wessex culture of Stonehenge, we may ponder what is lost and what still lies in the earth.

At the highest point of the hill is a large Bronze Age bell barrow, more prominent than the nearby bowl barrow, built when the causewayed enclosure was already two thousand years old. It is an excellent place to rest and admire the view. Windmill Hill is best viewed on cloudless days, in strong early morning or late afternoon sunlight, when the dips and banks in the ground are attenuated by the sharply angled light. In good sunlight, the circle of the inner ditch is visible to the immediate north east of the bell barrow.

From Windmill Hill, the great open spaces of Wessex are spread out as far as the eye can see. As you turn and turn about it seems as if the entire world is spread out at your feet. The magnificent outlook is the reason why the causewayed camp was constructed here. Once, its gleaming white banks of chalk would have been

Five Shamanic Landscapes

visible for many miles. On the ridge to the left is the line of the Ridgeway as it descends toward Avebury and the Sanctuary at Overton Down. In the vale below, Avebury and the great circle is largely concealed by trees, although a keen eye will be able to pick out the church and manor house. The great mound of Silbury Hill is unmistakable, and beyond it, lying low along the skyline, West Kennet long barrow can be made out on a clear day. A thousand years before Avebury, West Kennet long barrow and the camp at Windmill Hill were the only significant marks of human activity in the landscape.

The ditches at Windmill Hill have yielded a substantial assemblage of human bones, most too scattered to have been interred as complete skeletons. There is evidence that skulls and long bones were removed from West Kennet long barrow for ritual use at Windmill Hill.[16] This would have symbolized the presence of the ancestors at key rituals. Shamans use bones in divination. More significantly, the bones of a shaman may be preserved in order to retain his power once he has died and departed for the spirit world. It is widely believed that bodies were left to decompose on scaffolds in the Neolithic, pretty much as some Native American tribes did until very recent times. In one Asian culture this type of treatment was reserved for the bodies of shamans. The idea that these bodies were exposed to the elements and the sky in order to facilitate the release of the soul makes sense, given the prevalence of the belief amongst people who practice excarnation.[17] Keiller also uncovered a rectangular enclosure, at Windmill Hill, defined by a trench, which would have provided the foundations for a palisade. Within the palisade were many post-holes. It resembled the remains of a mortuary enclosure, which would have been used for the exposure of corpses, whilst the elements and scavenging animals defleshed them. This would have been a fearful place, entered perhaps by the priest or the shaman, and the focus of many rituals in its own right.

Windmill Hill was too large to be the work of a single clan. In the early Neolithic, a typical community might have numbered forty souls. Some see their arrival in the landscape as evidence of the emergence of powerful chieftains. It has also been suggested that such figures may have been a kind of priest-king – hence the disproportionate energy devoted to ritual monuments.[17] Under such a leader a number of communities would have worked together to enclose this space. It is probable that the enclosure would have been busy at times of seasonal rituals and fairs. Evidence suggests that autumn was the main period of occupation. During autumn, it would have been necessary to slaughter surplus livestock before the winter set in. Scrapers show that hides were prepared and the cut marks on bones and the splitting of long bones to extract marrow speaks of the accompanying feasting. The ancestral spirits would have been invited to these ritual feasts, as they still were at the Celtic festival of Samhain, three thousand years later. Windmill Hill also offers evidence of the use of the ditches as a medium for making ritual offerings. Complete animals

Five Shamanic Landscapes

have been found in the ditches, as well as carefully disposed heaps of bones that do not show the telltale bone cuts associated with consumption. The careful burial of such heaps of bones would imply ritual and sacrifice.

The archaeological evidence indicates that the ditches were regularly re-cut during the lifetime of the monument. Possibly the builders liked to keep the banks and ditches gleaming white, just as white horses on chalk downlands are maintained today.

It is only as I leave Windmill Hill, and follow the hedge-line path down toward the River Kennet and the Manor House that I am reminded of why Windmill Hill has become one of my special spaces. A few hundred metres from Windmill Hill, the drone of the traffic on the A4361 is audible and the modern world returns. Avebury stone circle has a busy road running right through it, whilst Silbury Hill and the Sanctuary are both cheek by jowl with the even busier A4 to Marlborough, where the constant intrusion of speeding traffic makes connection with the past all but impossible.

My path back to Avebury lies to the east of Windmill Hill heading toward the A4361. A gentle descent leads to the River Kennett and a path that follows the flow of the river to Avebury. We are walking on some of the oldest farms in the land, comparable with the farming communities of Salisbury Plain or the Boyne Valley in Ireland, whose settled prosperity gave men the wealth to build spectacular monuments.

The path to Avebury is level and easy. It crosses a narrow overgrown wood called Sloe Copse. Here a tiny, ancient stone footbridge crosses a winterbourne. From Sloe Copse there are a further two fields to cross and I am back in Avebury. I like to vary the route back to the monument and use the kissing gate that leads through the churchyard of St. James. The church is pretty and possesses a fine lychgate – of late nineteenth century provenance. The whole is a reminder of a different kind of sacred architecture and the coming of a different God to these lands. In the South West we are fortunate that some of the old ways have survived through the good offices of Mother Church. The old gods took new identities as Christian saints. Holy wells and sacred sites are consecrated anew to the Crucified. Nothing changes much. The old needs and fears are still there. Names may change but not the archetypes of the human subconscious they reflect, or the needs they serve.

It is time to walk to the companion monument of Windmill Hill – West Kennet long barrow.

The path to West Kennett begins on the opposite side of the road to the main car park entrance. Once across the busy road, the path follows the Kennett. A

Five Shamanic Landscapes

Silbury Hill, from the river Kennet, west of Avebury

fenced path runs north south alongside the river, and we have the fine combination of the water's gentle flow and the huge, impressive truncated cone of Silbury Hill ahead. Silbury Hill is a curious monument. Part of the hill is natural, created by cutting a spur of higher ground from its connecting hill. I cannot help but feel that the flooding that sees Silbury Hill surrounded by water at wet times of year was a deliberate phenomenon so reminiscent of the Primordial Mounds of Egyptian temple precincts. I am not suggesting that one culture influenced the other. Rather, the primordial mound reflects the innate form within our souls. It is part of an inner landscape manifested out there by human creativity. This strange hill is a shaman's dream and there we must travel to know its meaning.

Silbury does not contain a burial, and therefore the reason for its building remains a mystery. Michael Dames, in his book, 'The Silbury Treasure'[19], identified the hill as a "landform image of the Neolithic pregnant goddess,". His book, and it's sequel, 'The Avebury Cycle'[20], were timely books, drawing on the feminization of much of the alternative cultural scene. A sensible argument slowly becomes absurd, however, as his sequel goes on to find vulvas everywhere, including a contorted 'pit goddess' at my beloved Windmill Hill. He fails to answer one crucial question. In the Eastern European Neolithic, clearly defined images of the goddess are common. It seems crazy to propose an identical tradition for Avebury, when not a single

Five Shamanic Landscapes

goddess cult image has been found. Quite simply – and I regard the evidence as incontrovertible- the religious beliefs of the Neolithic of the western European seaboard were substantially different from those of Eastern Europe. The most cursory examination of surviving artifacts and ritual architecture demonstrates this. Michael Dames attempt to relate everything to the Goddess theme distorts the archaeological reality.

Silbury Hill has recently been subjected to extensive research, following the collapse of an old excavation shaft in May 2000. The Duke of Northumberland had tunnelled from the top to the bottom of the mound in 1776 and it was his excavation shaft that was exposed. He, like so many tomb-robbers, dreamt of treasure. Happily, what secrets Silbury Hill holds it has kept. May it always be so.

Recent research includes a thorough geophysics and topographic survey of the entire hill. One of the surprises was that the stepped profile of Silbury appears to be a spiral. If this were the case, it would seem that ritual ascent was intended. This would make Silbury similar to Ziggurats or Aztec pyramids, where ritual ascent led to the home of the gods. Such architecture has its origins in the primordial shamanistic mythology of the Cosmic Mountain. The advances of science give us a vision of what the shaman beheld – not a womb but a Cosmic Mountain, with a carefully constructed spiral path that led to its summit. [21]

It seems something of a mystery that the immense circle of Avebury and the equally impressive Silbury Hill should be build on low-lying ground – unlike the older monuments of Windmill Hill and West Kennett long barrow, where prominence seems to have been the important issue. I have little doubt that sanctity attached itself to the moist and fertile lower ground, and the presence of the rivers and springs added the kind of reverence associated with springs and running water amongst ancient cultures. Springs are a rarity on high ground in chalk country and the focus of ritual activity associated with fertility would always have been in the valleys.

The path to Silbury Hill follows the flow of the River Kennet, and once the A4361 is crossed and the road left behind, provides a beautiful and tranquil walk. The river flows lazily by, never more than a few yards away, as it makes its own way to Silbury and beyond, crossing the path to West Kennett long barrow, before following its valley east toward the Sanctuary. It will remain our companion until we climb the slopes of Overton Hill to view the Sanctuary and the Ridgeway.

The path brings us close to Silbury Hill, which we may admire from across the Kennet. But the A4 to Chippenham is now close. This is a mad, bad road, where

Five Shamanic Landscapes

Standing stones block the entrance to West Kennett long barrow

the modern obsession with speed is exercised to the full. There is a parking area on the far side of the road and the path to West Kennett Long Barrow is well sign-posted. The fenced path crosses the Kennet before heading in a straight line up the gentle slope of the down to the barrow.

West Kennett is a long, low, broken-backed mound of chalk. Its hundred metre length is difficult to appreciate and any beauty it may have had has been destroyed by the predations of the cart-track that once ran across it. Its fame lies in the stone structures the mound contains, with its symmetry of five, beautifully formed burial chambers that contained their precious charge of ancestral bones until 1955, when Professor Stuart Piggott and Professor R.J.C. Atkinson carried out a thorough excavation. They found the remains of at least forty-six people – men, women and children. The pottery remains indicate that it may have been the tomb of a ruling family, who used the tomb for a thousand years. This ties its history with that of Windmill Hill, with both monuments passing out of use in a similar period. The great megaliths you see at the entrance are not part of the original design. They form part of the sealing of the tomb at the end of its life. This sealing saw the tomb filled with earth, and the roof slighted to prevent future access. It is clear, however, that the ancestors were not deserted thereafter. The erection of the twelve foot high megaliths at its entrance indicates that it remained a place of ritual, in which the power of the ancestors could be summoned.

Five Shamanic Landscapes

I have visited West Kennett Long Barrow on many occasions and only once had the privilege of having the tomb to myself. It is a popular stopping off point for passing tourists and on busy days there is a steady procession of folk up and down the path to the barrow. I like to believe that the ancestors enjoy all this attention. Despite the removal of their bones (they were, after all, used to this happening), I am sure their spirits linger. They receive many an offering to sustain them. Flowers, incense and candles are common offerings, along with the many dawn and evening rituals that take place here. The ancestors are probably as confused as I am by the plethora of beliefs expressed by the faithful but I am sure they receive their offerings in good faith. As a place of worship it is probably better attended than some local churches. Not bad after five thousand years.

To continue the walk it is necessary to return to the Kennet. Shortly before the new bridge over the river, a stile gives access to a path that follows the river east to Overton Hill. The river has many moods. I have seen it bone dry and I have seen it deep and murky. Today it runs as clear as spring water and a family of swans idle their way back to Avebury against the gentle flow. Just after the bridge the bridleway continues to the right and we follow the tree-lined hedge, beyond which flows the river. Our path turns left at this point, to follow the hedge up the slope of Overton Hill to the Sanctuary. Barrows mark the approach to the sanctuary. A fine stone circle once stood on this hill.

Nothing remains of the Sanctuary now, except concrete markers, indicating where the ancient wooden postholes of the monument were found. The sense of loss is compounded by the overwhelming traffic noise, as lorries hurtle past at absurd speeds. Stukeley saw the stone circle of the Sanctuary virtually intact, before a farmer destroyed it in 1724. Long before the stone circle was built there appears to have been a large, circular hut, generally held to have been a charnel house. Large quantities of human remains were found here, pointing further to the association of the Sanctuary with death rites.

As you stand in the Sanctuary, you can see the concrete markers that indicate where the avenue of stones began that led to the heart of the Avebury complex over a mile and a half away. Today we can only imagine the stones and the ritual passage of the ancestors from the Sanctuary to the great circle at Avebury.

Whatever remained of the wooden building at the time of the building of the Avebury complex, this sacred place was clearly very important. Five thousand years ago an enormous amount of effort was made in erecting the hundreds of stones that link the Sanctuary to Avebury Stone Circles. Aubrey Burl describes how modern attempts to raise the stones give some insight into the labour involved:

Five Shamanic Landscapes

"In an experiment using prehistoric equipment, but with the security of steel cables, twelve men under the direction of an experienced foreman, managed to put up a smallish sarsen of about eight tons in five days. As nearly all the stones at Avebury weigh much more than this and are of awkward shape and bulk, and as originally in the circle and avenues there were some six hundred of these sarsens, we are once again given a glimpse of the appalling demands this monument made on the primitive society that constructed it."[22]

With the movement of stones weighing up to fifty tons being dragged considerable distances, and the building of a conical mound as grand as many of the pyramids of Egypt, we realize that we are dealing with a culture that could command and direct huge resources for the time. That so much effort should be expended to a religious purpose bespeaks the absence of committed spirituality in our own age.

Across the busy A4 is the Ridgeway. No doubt the positioning of the Sanctuary at this point was a deliberate act at so significant a location. Today, the Sanctuary marks the 'official' starting point of the long-distance National Trail, known as the Ridgeway, that takes you east to Tring, near London. In the opposite direction, the Ridgeway continues to Stonehenge and beyond. Sadly, only fragments of the ancient road have survived from here on, although there is talk of restoring the seventeen miles of path that take you to Stonehenge.

As we begin the ascent of the Ridgeway, we move on to a different age. The barrows are the prestige burial places of the Beaker People, so called because of the fine pottery beakers that often accompany their mortal remains to the afterlife. Bronze and gold artifacts have been found in their tombs. Most are individual burials of important individuals, who chose ancient and sacred locales for their last resting-place. Unlike their predecessors, their tombs were sealed. The transition is interesting. The long barrows of the Neolithic are believed to reflect the longhouses of the living. The circular dwellings of the Early Bronze Age likewise seem to be reflected in tomb architecture. No longer are the bones of the dead accessible and this has been interpreted as marking a transition in religious beliefs from the worship of ancestors to gods of the earth and the sky. The countless spirits that inhabit the rocks, the streams, the trees and the animals are named and become deities. This was, perhaps the shaman's twilight, with the ascendancy of a priesthood. The great temples of stone erected at Stonehenge and Avebury ceased to be places where the shaman danced and drummed. The shaman has no place in the courts of kings. Shamanism, like Wicca, is the religion of common folk. He is on the outside now, amidst the squalid huts and middens of Windmill Hill and the

Five Shamanic Landscapes

decaying forecourts of the long barrows. He represented the Old Religion when the great stones of Avebury were new.

The round barrows overlooking Avebury are particularly beautiful in the late afternoon sun. Many are crowned with trees, which radiate from the barrow in an arc, creating a graceful canopy. The roots have wrapped themselves around the bones of the long dead and guard them from desecration by the living. A tomb stripped bare of bones is a sad thing. How can the spirits be summoned when their remains sit in cardboard boxes on the shelves of museums and universities?

The Ridgeway itself is undoubtedly a spirit path. How could a road that has been walked for five thousand years not carry the souls of those who came here? This was the path to the West, trod by the Celts, the Romans, the Saxons, Vikings and Norman alike. All of Albion's history lies beneath your feet. So do the footsteps of the shaman.

If you choose to follow the stone avenue leading into Avebury the path bears left to take us past those mysterious tree-covered barrows, where, on a winter's eve, you can sense the stirring of the barrow wraiths as the sun sets and the world turns to darkness. It is a very powerful spot, built where the dead wait upon the sounding of the drum. We walk past in silence, paying our respects with a small libation of milk and honey and cross the field in a line that reflects where the stones once were. At the roadside, we come to the first surviving stones that straddle the road to Avebury. A stile on the far side provides access to the field in which the great avenue of stones will guide us to the heart of Avebury.

Avebury is not a single monument but a complex. Some of it belongs to the Shaman, whilst the gigantic circle at its heart may well bespeak his decline. However we choose to read these monuments, I have no doubt that its 'grand plan' reflected an ancient sanctity that goes back to the Time of the Shaman. His paths and his dancing ground in the courts of the ancestors were the inspiration for all that followed. Even here, we must strip away the layers to the time of woods and streams, where Nature alone monumentalized the landscape. The shaman's penetration of the earth and ascent to the sky affirmed the reality of that great axis of energy that binds all things. What followed was an affirmation in stone of the most sacred pathways on earth, where the ancestors still walked and the shaman wrought a power that held the world in balance.

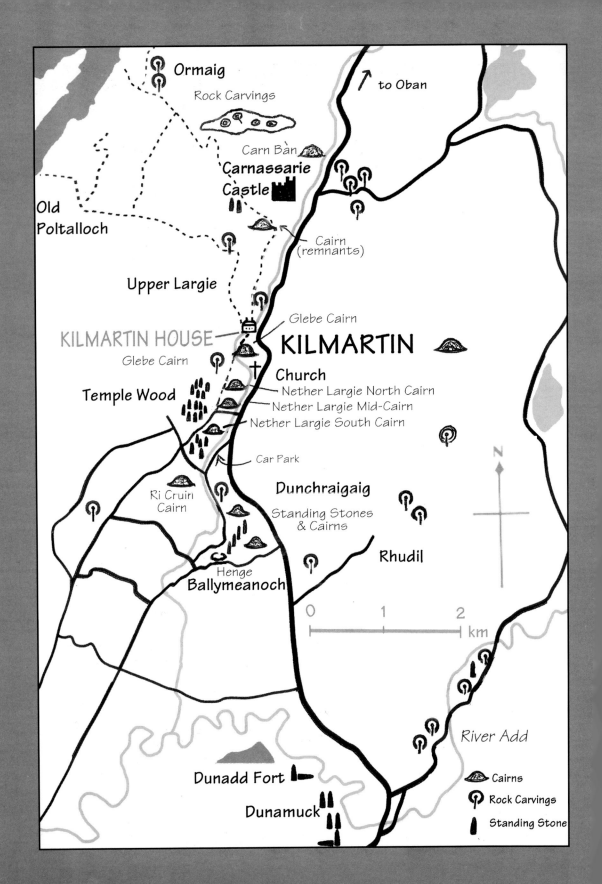

Shamanism and Sacred Landscapes

Five Shamanic Landscapes

4.3. Kilmartin Glen
'The Valley of Ghosts'

It was on a pilgrimage to Iona that I first stumbled upon Kilmartin Glen. This quiet valley, with its village pub, church, and scatter of houses struggles to persuade the tourist to break his journey to Oban and the Isles. The driver in a hurry will miss the alignments of standing stones and the solemn grey burial cairns that march down the glen towards the sea. Certainly, he will see nothing of the great slabs of living rock, covered in the most elaborate and mysterious carvings. Stop, get out of the car, and all that changes. What overwhelms the visitor, who is prepared to give Kilmartin Glen the time it deserves, is the sheer weight of its past. Modernity lies thinly on the landscape and for those who care to walk its quiet lanes and forest walks, it is the shaman's voice they will hear. They call it 'the Valley of Ghosts', for everywhere is the insistent presence of the dead.

Standing stones, Ballymeanoch, Kilmartin Glen

Kilmartin Glen nestles between fine, wooded hills, close to the western coast of Scotland. The proximity to the sea is not apparent from the glen, but from the hills above the village of Kilmartin you can look across the Sound of Jura to the islands of Islay, Jura, Colonsay and Oronsay. The glen itself shelves gently towards the marshes of Moine Mhor and the sea at Loch Crinan. Standing sentinel at the mouth of Kilmartin Glen and guarding the road to the sea is the great rock of Dunadd Fort from whose bastions the kings of Strathclyde brought all of Scotland under their dominion in the days of the Viking incursions.

The Glen has a flat, often damp valley floor, given over to arable use. To the sides of the valley floor are level terraces that appear artificial in nature. In fact, the glen is the product of glaciation. The terraces are the result of gravel deposits from glaciers that formed on Rannoch Moor and the corries of Ben Cruachan during the last Ice Age. Ten thousand years ago glacial meltwaters were still flowing through Kilmartin Glen, depositing substantial gravel terraces,

Five Shamanic Landscapes

including the one on which Kilmartin village now stands. Not long after the retreat of the ice, hunter-gatherers made seasonal use of the inlets and coastal areas in their annual round of hunting and fishing. Excavations on the nearby island of Oronsay have revealed a wealth of evidence of Mesolithic settlement and the remains of a Mesolithic bone harpoon was found at Oban. In Kilmartin no direct evidence from the Mesolithic has been found – evidence of human activity begins with the Neolithic. What greets the visitor to Kilmartin is one of the most important Neolithic and Bronze Age ritual landscapes in the British Isles.

The famous Temple Wood stone circles, and the Neolithic Nether Largie Cairn are signposted from the Oban road and, at the height of the tourist season, attract the casual visitor en route to the Isles. During the long, summer afternoons, children play happily on the ancient cairns, trying out the cists for size that once contained the bones of kings. Some may notice the cup and ring markings on the standing stones, the worn outlines of axe heads on cists, and the astonishing carvings on nearby rock outcrops, which are the greatest treasure of this valley. The sheer quantity of the prehistoric remains was revealed by the patient work of an amateur archaeologist, Marion Campbell, who in the 1960s recorded 640 ancient monuments in the valley and the surrounding hills. Increasingly, archaeologists see the phenomenon of Kilmartin Glen as much more than the product of a slow accretion of monuments. Kilmartin is a unity, where carved rocks define the boundaries of this sacred space, and each cairn is raised with due respect to what was built before. Understanding this unity is the key to comprehending what it all means. This is Scotland's Avebury, where the sheer numbers of ritual monuments are too many to have served a single community. As with Avebury, this was probably a ritual centre for many communities, who came here at significant times of the year to perform the great seasonal rituals, do business, marry, bury their dead, and shamanize. The most visible set of monuments in the valley is the linear cemetery of cairns that originated in the Neolithic and continued to be built throughout the Bronze Age.

Linear cemeteries of cairns or barrows are typical of the Bronze Age. That they often align on much earlier monuments, such as ancient Long Barrows or chambered tombs is also common. Such practices demonstrate the reverence of later generations for the sacred sites of their forbears. The change of funeral practices in the Bronze Age must reflect a change of beliefs, and yet there is no doubt they regarded the ancient remains they found in the landscape as especially sacred. The Neolithic stone circles at Temple Wood and the chambered tomb at Nether Largie South were transformed hundreds of years after they were first built. Bronze Age cist burials were inserted in both these monuments and their shape altered to match that of the later Bronze Age cairns. The power of the Ancestors survives through all ages.

Five Shamanic Landscapes

Nature has helped to preserve these monuments by covering much of what you see in peat when the climate cooled in the latter years of the Iron Age. The Duns or forts that dot the hills are a consequence of the struggle for survival that followed the slow disappearance of cultivatable land. In the eighteenth century, the Highland clearances saw landlords forcing the crofters off the land in order to farm sheep. The result was the creation of a wilderness on the higher ground. This also helped to preserve the monuments from the depredations of modernity. During the nineteenth century, however, the process was reversed and farmers began the backbreaking work of cutting away millennia of peat to reclaim the fertile soils beneath. They ended up exposing a land that had not seen the light of day for three thousand years. Some of the cairns were robbed at this stage to provide stones for roads and field drains.

Kilmartin has an award-winning museum, which provides an evocative introduction to the valley. From the museum you can literally step out into the landscape and visit the majority of the monuments on foot, without the disturbance of modern traffic. An old coach road runs alongside the linear cemetery and the majority of tombs and stone settings can be accessed from it. The modern visitor can follow the journey of the shaman in his flight across this landscape of the dead. For those with stout shoes and modest map-reading skills, more remote monuments can be visited by walking through the forest plantations that crown the hills. Here, peace and privacy can be found for those who might wish to enter the mindscapes of those ancient men and women, whose mysterious rock carvings of pierced rings and cup marks create gateways into the earth.

Our journey begins at Kilmartin House, which is now the Museum of Ancient Culture. Visiting the main monuments is best done early in the morning or late in the evening. Scottish summers give long days and an early morning or evening start will give you the monuments to yourself. From the museum I walk beside the Oban road towards Carnassarie Castle, before taking the path that can be accessed just before a tin-roofed garage a

Cup and ring markings, Baluachraig, Kilmartin Glen

Shamanism and Sacred Landscapes

Five Shamanic Landscapes

few hundred metres north of Kilmartin House. High above Carnassarie castle, and forming the northernmost of the cairns, is Carn Ban. Situated atop a great rocky hill, it provides an eagle's nest from which the entire valley can be surveyed. On a first journey, however, it is better to stay on the valley floor to allow time to absorb the atmosphere of the monuments that can be more readily accessed. Just before the garage is a kissing gate, which permits access to Glebe Cairn, which dominates the centre of the field behind the museum. As you approach the cairn there are striking views along the flat valley floor and the terraces to either side. From here, Nature provides a frame for the monuments - and the entire landscape can be perceived as a single entity, created by the terrible force of glacial torrents and focussed by the spirit of man. The cairn is made of a great heap of grey-white stones, around a hundred feet in diameter and nine feet high. Rev. Greenwell, a canon from Durham Cathedral, excavated it in 1864. He discovered two circular stone settings and two burial cists. A fine pottery vessel and a beautiful jet necklace were found.[23] It is likely that the original ritual monument, consisting of the stone settings and the cist, later incorporated a second cist before being covered with the great cairn. Glebe Cairn belongs to the Bronze Age and the older, Neolithic monuments lie further down the valley. We are travelling back from the time of the priest and king to the shaman of the wood circles. The apparent similarity in cairn design from the Neolithic through to the late Bronze Age is no accident. This monument was re-shaped, as was the Neolithic Cairn at Nether Largie, so that a simplicity and similarity of form would draw the eye and the soul. They form a rich pathway from which the shaman may follow the Ancestors onwards to the sea and the journey into the West.

Not far from Glebe Cairn is Kilmartin Burn. From Glebe Cairn the path leads to a little wooden bridge across the burn and the quiet lane that follows the line of the glen. Once across the bridge and on the path, Nether Largie North cairn can be seen in the near distance. In the absence of any distraction, movement from cairn to cairn becomes an act of meditation. This was once a processional route for the rituals that celebrated the Ancestors. In walking this quiet path, we are following the footsteps of the shaman priest of old who journeyed through this otherworldly landscape. In this great valley he walked to evoke the stored power of the ancestral spirits. Here lie the kings of old and on their blessing depends the very turning of the year. When ice and snow returns, and the land is locked in wintry death, the ancestors fly to the sun to beg its return. The whole equilibrium of the natural world is balanced within this landscape. The tombs, stone alignments, circles, and carved rocks are a focus of shamanic power. He dances and whirls in the approaching dusk until the veil falls away and the dead are there for those who have eyes to see. As the sun sets over the hills to the west, his presence overwhelms the soul. He is eternally present in the light and shadow of the fiery sunset.

Five Shamanic Landscapes

Close by Nether Largie Cairn is a cup-marked rock. Some of these ancient carvings are at least as old as the cairns and may well be older. They mark sacred locales and in this instance may have provided the reason for the siting of the cairn. I have often mused on how these cup-marked rocks might have been 'used'. There is evidence in the more heavily carved rocks that the carvings may have been made over long periods of time. Little attempt is made to achieve artistic coherence. The designs are usually repetitive and their positioning on the rock seemingly random. In its simplest form - the cup – a hemisphere of about three or four inches in diameter and depth, is ground out of the rock by what looks like a grinding circular motion. They are seen most clearly in strong, low sunlight or when rain has filled the hollows. The more complex versions have multiple rings around them. So, what do they mean?

The simplicity and repetitive nature of the pecking and grinding of cup and ring marks implies that the making process was in itself a 'spiritual' act – rather like the painting of Icons in the Orthodox Church. Over whatever span of history these carvings were made there was little by way of artistic innovation. As with Icons or Egyptian tomb carvings, the sacred forms were an inherited tradition. As more carvings appeared and they became the work of the ancestors, they would also become repositories of spiritual power. They are strange things –going back to a time when natural features were held in awe. Yet, they express the desire of humankind to alter the physical landscape to reflect the landscape of the imagination. Such acts – the carving of the living rock or the building of a cairn – unite these inner and outer worlds and are essentially shamanic.

Cup and ring markings, Ormaig, near Kilmartin Glen

The cairn at Nether Largie North has been reconstructed, built to protect the burial cist that lies at the heart of the original monument. The ruined cairn was excavated in 1930 by Joseph Craw, who found a low bank surrounding a central cist.[24] There were also two small standing stones, one bearing carved rings. This stone is now part of the display at Kilmartin House. The reconstructed cairn contains a chamber, accessed from above. Inside is a large cist, which once held the body of a high status member of his community. Excarnation (where only the skull

Shamanism and Sacred Landscapes

Five Shamanic Landscapes

and larger bones are placed in the tomb following decomposition) had passed out of use when this tomb was built and it is likely that a complete body was placed in this stone coffin. The massive lid of the cist is now propped against the wall and the stone is covered in carvings of axe-heads and cup-marks. The back wall of the cist also has two axe-heads carved into its surface.

The cup marks appear older than the axe-head carvings and may well be an example of an older sacred object being re-used and dedicated to the chieftain with new symbols of power and prestige. It is possible that the number of axes were meant to reflect the wealth of the chieftain or perhaps the number of fighting men under his command.

Beyond Nether Largie North cairn is Nether Largie Mid cairn. Here the cairn stands in its ruinous state. Sadly, this ruination is a modern event, and the cairn was virtually intact as recently as 1920. This means that at least 160 generations of farmers had respected this sacred space. Now the cairn lies robbed, probably to provide materials for road building. Times have changed, and we are part of an age where the absence of a relationship with landscape – and through landscapes our ancestors – means that we have no stake in the sacred. Some of the original kerbstones can still be seen and to the southern edge of the cairn one of the two cists the cairn contained lies exposed. The large triangular shaped capstone has been propped open with bronze supports so that the interior of the cist can be examined. The second cist lies buried beneath the surface of the cairn towards the centre. On the inner surface of the NW end slab there is at least one cupmark. Look for it. There is a special joy in finding hidden things.

We may reflect on this ruin, stripped and despoiled to provide materials for modern development. Clearly, the landowner cared little for such things. There was a further cairn between Nether Largie Mid cairn and Nether Largie South. This has vanished completely and survives only as a shadow in the grass. Thankfully, the monuments further down the valley have fared better.

Nether Largie South is the oldest surviving cairn in the alignment. Access to the tomb is along a path just to the south of Kilmartin Primary School. Its structural difference from the other cairns is immediately apparent, being a chambered tomb. Built for the communal burial of the dead, it has a long narrow chamber constructed with large stone slabs. The tomb is aligned NE and SW, meaning that the entrance was aligned on the rising sun. This sacred space can be entered, but it is wise to visit early in the morning or late in the evening, as it can become rather busy during the tourist season. It can be distressing to watch children using our ancient monuments as playgrounds. These places do belong to everyone. At the same time, they belong to the future as well, and the careless attitude of many visitors takes its toll. The last two centuries have done more

Five Shamanic Landscapes

damage to our Stone Age and Bronze Age monuments than the previous 4000 years, reflecting a society that has lost its spirituality. A sense of awe and wonder in the presence of something so old and so powerful, and respect for our ancestors are all reasons why this tomb survived for nearly two hundred generations. For countless centuries, it remained a focus for ceremony and celebration, even when their original purpose was lost. Today, they are used for religious purposes by a few and otherwise dug over to support someone's doctoral thesis, and ignored or abused by the casual visitor. The idea of the holy is lost to many and with its loss a whole dimension of human experience has vanished away.

Nether Largie South once had the more traditional shape of a trapezoidal long barrow – typical of what is known as the 'Clyde' style. There may also have been a 'horn work' to either side of the entrance, providing a ritual space in which the shaman would have communicated with the dead. These ceremonial spaces focussed on the tomb entrance and are a feature of many tombs dating to the Neolithic. Excavation usually reveals evidence of fire pits, indicative of night ceremonies and ritual feasting. In some instances, there is evidence of cremations, perhaps to speed up the de-fleshing of bones prior to burial, or, as is still the case in Hinduism, to help release the soul from its now useless mortal cage.

When you look into the tomb, you do not see the original ground level. The septal slabs that divide the floor into four chambers once stood nearly a metre high, whereas all we see now are the tops of the stones. These slabs served the dual purpose of dividing the tomb into separate spaces and providing bracing for the uprights. The design has stood the test of time. Two portal stones and a sealing slab now guard the entrance and it is necessary to drop a little way down to the floor. At the back of the chamber there appears to be some kind of seat. The practical function of this stone appears to be to brace the two large slabs that form the wall of the chamber at this point. I have seen similar structures in tombs in Orkney, where they possibly served a ritual function.

Protected by the gravel beneath your feet are a series of burial deposits of cremated bones and that

entrance to Nether Largie South chambered cairn

Shamanism and Sacred Landscapes

Five Shamanic Landscapes

'unctuous dark earth', which is all that remains of our flesh and blood once we have laid in the earth awhile. The presence in the tomb of beaker style food vessels and tanged and barbed arrowheads indicates that the burial chamber was opened again and re-used in the Bronze Age, possibly several hundred years after the original Neolithic burials. The Bronze Age beakers found in the cairn are of an early type, indicating that this may well have been the earliest monument to be used by the beaker people. Nether Largie South was possibly the only cairn in the valley at the beginning of the Bronze Age and may have provided the inspiration for the linear cemetery that followed. The appearance of these vessels and the change in burial practice indicate a transition of belief. The shaman would still have his part to play, but his role in acting as intermediary with the ancestors was probably no longer central to this society. Cist and cairn burials are becoming an expression of status, rather than a critical tool in maintaining the equilibrium between the worlds of the living and the dead. Our Bronze Age forebears also

Standing stones, Carnassarie, Kilmartin Glen

built two cists into this cairn. One you may lie in, if you wish (as various children did on the date of my last visit), with the weighty capstone propped open above you. At its zenith, this was possibly the most impressive of the cairns in the linear cemetery, being as much as forty metres across. It is a good place to meditate on your own mortality, but don't forget to leave a simple offering of mead or milk for its original occupant.

As we continue our walk of the dead down this old coaching road we come to one of the most fascinating and strange monuments of all – Temple Wood stone circles, 250 metres to the SW of Nether Largie South. Standing in a fine copse of mature trees, Temple wood can be full of atmosphere in its quieter moments. I am always astonished at how quickly the calm and sanctity of this place asserts itself. The circles date back to the earliest period of Neolithic occupation. Excavation revealed evidence of a wooden henge monument that pre-dates the stone circles you now see. The first stone

Five Shamanic Landscapes

circle – the smaller of the two rings, occupies the site of the original wooden circle. This is, therefore, the oldest standing monument in the glen. It would seem that construction was not completed before work began on the more ambitious main circle. Originally it was free of all the cairn stones – it was a stone circle, pure and simple. The ground on which the rituals took place in the Neolithic was buried gradually during the Bronze Age as cists were inserted into the sacred earth and covered with cairns. Over time the cairns merged to become the monument you see today. Temple Wood is a superb example of the perceived sacredness of place. Time moves on, religious beliefs change, but it is to the most ancient of places that generations came to bury their dead and perform their more potent rituals. This stone circle was literally buried by the reverence of future generations. Stone circles are predominantly a phenomenon of the Bronze Age. The origins of this stone circle, however, lie in the Time of the Shaman, and the wooden henges built by hunter-gatherers to contain the spirits of the dead.

Several more cairns remain in this great linear cemetery. Sadly, only one more can be visited without returning to the busy A816. This walk ends with the wonderful cairn at Ri Cruin. Situated by a fine, old farmhouse, which offers outstanding bed and breakfast facilities, this cairn stands in a copse of mature trees at the end of a beautiful path. The path itself is lawned and green, indicative of how few people seek it out. Sadly, the cairn is partly despoiled, mainly through the robbing of its stones in the nineteenth century. The mound was also home to a lime kiln in previous centuries. The tranquil space in which the cairn stands is evocative, and the two visible cists of this cairn reward the visitor with fine ancient carvings. The southernmost cist has a back wall carved with at least eight axe-heads. Axes may well be a local symbol of wealth. Copper was available locally as an ore, but the tin to alloy it would have had to be imported from considerable distances. Copper mines lie within one mile of Kilmartin, but tin would have to be brought from Cornwall and paid for accordingly.

As well as axe-heads, a carved stone was found with an enigmatic design that has yet to be deciphered. The most northerly cist, which is orientated NNE by SSW, possesses a huge capstone and probably contained the primary burial. To the south of the cairn is another complete cist, and this is decorated with carved axe heads. The slabs of a third, ruined cist lie close by. The cairn has been partially restored and the evidence of the lime kiln removed.

The return to Kilmartin is accomplished by continuing along the lane east past Ri Cruin and turning left to walk the short distance to the Nether Largie stone alignments and back to the old coach road. The Nether Largie stones offer a mystery of alignments, as well as cup and ring carvings. There are two pairs of stone alignments, approximately seventy metres apart, with their axis

Shamanism and Sacred Landscapes

Five Shamanic Landscapes

orientated NE and SW. In the middle of them are two settings of four and five stones respectively, which share the same alignment. The southernmost stone and the large central stone in the cluster of four, both carry cup marks. It becomes apparent that the NE and SW alignment predominates in Kilmartin. This is perhaps not surprising, as this is the alignment of the entire glen. Once more, we see the builders of ancient monuments working in harmony with nature, reflecting the forces that shaped their lives. As for the cairns we have visited, the edge of a ruler placed on an OS map will pass through the centre of all four surviving cairns, demonstrating the care taken to focus the power our ancestors sought to generate in this valley. Standing between the two alignments at Nether Largie and looking back along the valley to the rock on which Carn Ban stands, the entire cemetery falls within the alignment, stressing the argument that we are dealing with something that was ultimately conceived as a single entity. To what end?

Standing stones, Ballymeanoch, Kilmartin Glen

In truth, we can only guess at the meaning behind the form. That there is cosmological significance is sure, for the arrangement of stones with the rising and setting sun or with lunar events is apparent. That they connect with what lies beneath us is also apparent, for tombs provide entrances to the underworld and the Land of the Dead. Linearity provides a visual focus, and, as with cursus monuments or stone rows, a defined path that we of the Middle World must follow. The path joins all three worlds and therefore symbolizes the polar axis of the shaman's universe.

There are three further cairns a few hundred metres further on from Ri Cruin and the stone alignments at Nether Largie, but these do not form part of the near perfect alignment as they veer off the SW axis. The reason for this change of alignment is easily apparent. At Ballymeanoch, where the cairns are clustered, is a distinct ritual landscape of stone alignments, cairns, carved rocks and henge monument. To get to these monuments it is safer to travel by car along the A816 to the car park at Dunchraigaig, as a pavement is not provided and field boundaries prevent access across open countryside.

Five Shamanic Landscapes

Ballymeanoch is a complete sacred landscape in itself, with the most beautiful views you could wish for. It is approached by way of the cairn of Dunchraigaig, which is in a copse at the roadside. A path gives access to a large field in which is situated a second cairn, a henge monument and an alignment of standing stones, one richly marked with cup and ring carvings. The henge monument is now largely destroyed and dates back to the Neolithic. It is unique to the west of Scotland, being the only henge monument in this part of Britain. The standing stones form two parallel alignments, one being of four stones and the other of two. They are positioned NW-SE, corresponding roughly to the rising and setting of the sun. One stone from these settings is now missing, having fallen in the nineteenth century. As with the stones at Nether Largie, we can speculate endlessly on the meaning of their form and orientation. For me, the meaning lies in the experience of the stones, rather than in any formal analysis. So fine are the stones, so redolent of a past in all their decayed splendour, that simply to be with them is enough. They are immensely photogenic, being set like jewels in this beautiful landscape. It is a mechanical thing to photograph them, and yet to struggle with their form, as the camera requires, at least helps you to internalise what the stones have to say.

Modern interpretations of these monuments tend to reflect our materialist values – with dissection by scientists, educative reconstruction and boards to provide a potted account of the material remains. As to the beliefs of the builders – well, that is another matter. That this was a sacred landscape is something that is difficult to define for the modern mind. 'The burial of the dead' indicates a practical function, 'grave goods' indicate wealth and the carvings the status of the individuals who sleep within the cairns. Our dowsers, crystal gazers and pagans have also got it wrong, imposing their own idea of sanctity on places whose original meaning is as lost as the lives of those who built them. How can we draw on the power of place with honesty?

With integrity and an open heart is the answer. These monuments, from their first inception, meant something different to all who came to them. The cist monuments inserted into the earlier Neolithic structures undoubtedly reflect a profound change of belief, but not, I believe, of sentiment. Sanctity is born of the unconscious. It is the pre-rational response that Otto calls 'the numinous'. The shamanic technique provides our best way forward to appreciate these landscapes with honesty. We impose nothing of the rational on them but wait for them to speak to us. We let the experiences flow and only when this is done should we permit our rational selves to ask what they mean. The mystic and the ecstatic are not dealing with words but with the numen. Like love, this cannot be shared with words alone. You must experience it for yourself and only then will you know the truth. This is the truth of the shaman and it cannot come from words or books.[25]

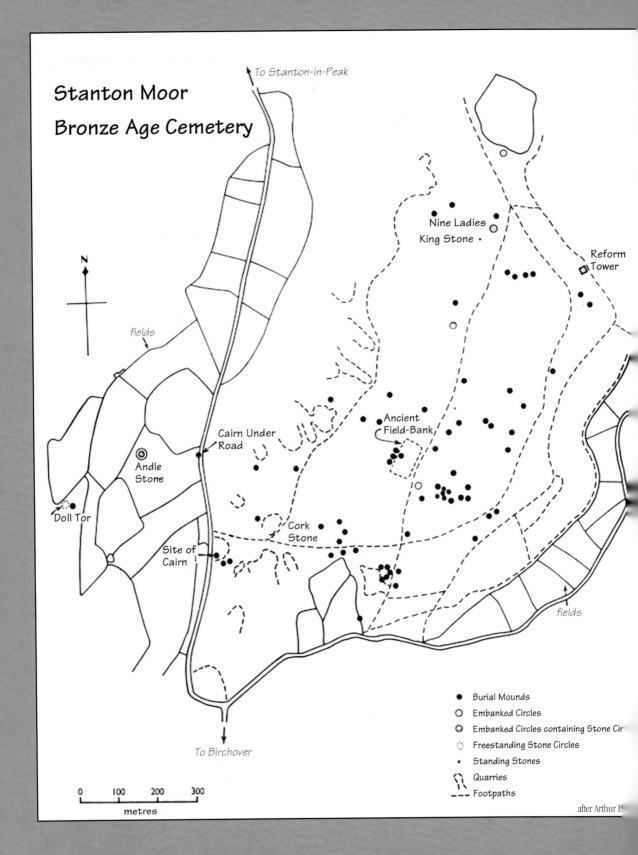

Five Shamanic Landscapes

4.4. Spirits of the Stone
The Peak District

The Peak District, in the North West of England, was Britain's first National Park. The populations of several industrial cities – Manchester, Sheffield, Derby, Nottingham, Leeds, and Stafford are all within easy travelling distance of this beautiful landscape, making it a popular weekend destination. This area of bleak limestone moors, peat bogs, deep valleys, dramatic crags, woods and intimate farmland marks the southern terminus of the Pennines. The terrain varies from the bleakest of peat moor – which becomes impassable bog after heavy rain – and gentle, rolling farmland criss-crossed with a spider's web of ancient stone walls. The evidence for man's early settlement of the Peak dates back 50,000 years. Caves at Creswell Crags have yielded pieces of carved bone, depicting a reindeer, a human figure and a horse in the same style we see in the caves of the French Palaeolithic. The Peak also has a wealth of stone circles and barrows. None have the size of a Stonehenge or Avebury but many of these monuments are in locales undisturbed by busy roads and what they lack in spectacle they make up for in atmosphere.

I grew up in the shadow of the northern reaches of the Peak District, in an industrial town called Stockport. My childhood memories are of cobbled streets of grim terraced two-up, two downs, gas lights, buildings blackened with factory smoke and a skyline dominated by the tall chimney-stacks of old mills. Open countryside, was, however, never more than a bus or bicycle ride away, and the hills and moors were visible as dreamy vistas above and beyond the urban prison of my everyday life. The distant hills that I could see from my attic bedroom and through the mock gothic windows of my primary school classroom were the destination of my first shamanic flights and the Eden of my unnamed desires. Already, many years before I first heard the word 'shaman', my psychic survival was dependent on a flight of the soul.

A book I had picked up in an Oxfam shop provided me with my first introduction to Britain's prehistoric past. It was a gazetteer, with a section for each of the British counties, further subdivided into 'Palaeolithic', 'Neolithic', 'Bronze Age' and 'Iron Age'. Like many urban dwellers, this teenage schoolboy had no idea so much of our distant past had survived or what the remains looked like. This well-written and illustrated little book, by Nicholas Thomas, was to spark off a life-long quest to get closer to the past.[26]

It was thus that I came to know the antiquities of Derbyshire and Staffordshire, which in those days were accessible by train, bus and bicycle. My curiosity first lighted upon Arbor Low, a great beast of a henge monument, dating back to the Neolithic. The photograph provided by the book was taken from the air. To

Five Shamanic Landscapes

my untutored eye it looked like a lunar crater, ringed with great shards of stone. Nearby was a prominent round barrow named 'Gib Hill' so-called because it once bore the gibbet on which local criminals met their fate. I was sufficiently inspired to attempt a cold February pilgrimage to what was to become my first contact with prehistory.

It had been snowing in the days before I visited Arbor Low. In those days it was possible to put your bicycle in the guards van. I took train and bicycle to Buxton, a fine Georgian spa town in the heart of the Peak District. From there, I cycled the ten or so miles on that cold Saturday, along main roads and country lanes of ice and drifted snow, until a turning off the main road bore the sign for Arbor Low.

I have to confess this wasn't my first encounter with an 'Ancient Monument'. As a mere boy of seven I had come across a great brute of a chambered tomb at a place called Din Llgwy, whilst on a family holiday on the island of Anglesey. Close by were the ruins of a medieval church and a village dating back to the days of the Roman conquest. But I had no idea what it all meant and the spooky atmosphere of the place did no more than give me nightmares. Prehistory was not considered worth teaching children in those days, and I knew little of what lay between the 'cavemen' and Caesar's legions. And in my childhood, Caesar came just before Queen Victoria, whose pennies I carried in my pocket. Time compresses, in the childhood imagination and in the mature memory of later years. That first visit to Arbor Low is still as fresh as if it were yesterday.

I follow the country lanes until I find the grey, metal sign that discreetly advertised the 'Ancient Monument'. I leave the road to follow a messy snow-and sileage covered farm track. Some way up the track I come to a dilapidated collection of farm buildings. Perched on a chair by a door is a small plastic, lidless sandwich box with a few coins in it and a sign requesting payment for the privilege of visiting Arbor Low. A girl of thirteen or fourteen appears, leading a tethered goat. Beyond her, a large German Shepherd barks frantically, straining on its chain in my direction. I feel intimidated and drop a coin into the box. I pass beyond the farm buildings and walk towards a stile. Once over this, the farm buildings disappear below the slope of the ground. Ahead of me, two great crescents of earth curve outwards. I walk through the causeway in the great circle of earth banks and enter sacred ground.

I remember that leaden clouds hung low on the horizon that day, threatening to blanket the dark blue winter sky in which a crescent moon already shone. I hadn't expected such numbing cold. It was about two thirty in the afternoon and the short, early February day was almost over. Even with its covering of snow the great arcs of earth that encompass Arbor Low were of a scale I had not expected. They are still several feet high, creating a secret space within. The

Five Shamanic Landscapes

two causeways into the temple are aligned on the Midsummer sunset and the Midwinter sunrise, compressing time and space in their simple design. The stones are ringed about the space within the ditch and bank like roman numerals on a clock dial.

Scattered in a great circle, each stone is now recumbent, as if gradually sinking into the earth from which they came. Fallen perhaps, but still charged with their original mystery. I walk to the centre and stand upon one of the stones that mark the heart of the circle. For the first time, I notice that one of the stones has not quite fallen. It leans now at a sharp angle, as if descending slowly to earth. In my mind I see the countless centuries passing, with the stones gradually losing their strength and power and laying down to die. So slowly that generations pass as they descend. So slowly that people visit them as children and then as old folk and have not noticed their movement. They move earthwards, taking with them the memory of those who sacrificed blood and barley and first hauled the stones upright to face the heavens.

Arbor Low does not need its stones to impress, massive and weatherworn though they are. What impresses is a profound sense of the relationship of this great henge with the earth and the sky. As you turn and turn about, you realize that you can see for many miles in all directions. It feels like the hub of the earth, drawing in the rotational energies of the entire globe as it spins around this fixed point.

A man appears in bright orange waterproofs and a curiously coloured bobble-hat, which, along with his beard, conspires to hide most of his face. In tow, a girl of six or seven. He scans the circle. If he has any expression at all, it is one of disappointment. A camera is retrieved from the folds of orange plastic and a single photograph taken in my general direction. He and his daughter climb the high point in the ring of earth-works where a Bronze Age burial mound has been built on its crest. He takes a blue plastic sack from his pack. On this his daughter sits, holding the lower end up over her feet, and slides down the snow covered bank into the ditch below. She does not laugh or giggle. The man in the orange waterproofs talks quietly to her. It seems more like ritual than play, as if the poor child has been made to slide down snow banks all day and now does it simply to keep her father happy. Both get bored quickly and trek off towards Gib Hill, the barrow in the middle distance, to see if any excitement can be found there. Halfway they stop to look at the horses. The girl strokes a muzzle whilst the horse searches eagerly for tid-bits. The horse finds nothing and turns away. They have found nothing too, and, with their journey incomplete, turn back to trudge through the drifted snow towards the farm-buildings.

I stare for some time at the space that they occupied. Just discernable, along my line of vision is a low bank of earth, covered by snow, which marked the

Five Shamanic Landscapes

processional way that had once been built between the circle of Arbor low and the barrow now called Gib Hill. Five thousand years ago a great people processed along this way to the great circle and made their pacts, conducted business and wrought the magic that gave the illusion of security to their fragile world. My forbears five thousand years ago. My forbears. Their blood in my veins. Me, present in their loins. And I am here returned, to let them abide in my memory and live again through me.

Behind me, I feel the presence of someone. I turn round to see three walkers enter the circle. They are equipped for a long walk, and carry substantial packs that must contain tents and sleeping bags. They seem not to be interested in what lies about them. They walk through as if they have passed this way many times before. They grunt 'hi's' as they stride purposefully onwards, walking past me and through the processional entrance on the far side. I continue to watch them as they walk across the open fields. Strange figures they become in the distance. Headless hulks behind their packs, orange, green and red against the landscape. Eventually uneven blobs of colour, devoid of humanity, pop out of sight below a ridge and out of my life forever.

Then came the silence. A townie like me wasn't used to silence – certainly not silence without birds or animals or wind. I sat down on one of the fallen stones and waited. My fingers were so numb they'd stopped hurting and I was able to focus on the silence.

Words don't work when you want to explain those moments of vision. I made my first 'journey', even as I sat in my reverie on that bitter-cold day. I did not feel that I physically left where I sat – rather the space beyond seemed to pour into me. In the space were souls, thousands of them. Time fell away and briefly, I shared a forgotten time with all those who had come here, even to the beginning of time. That sense of that thin divide between the worlds of the living and the great well of ancestral souls has never left me. It is the divide that the shaman learns to cross in his night of destruction.

None of it added up to anything extraordinary. But that overwhelming sense of another reality was to keep me coming back to the places that I felt might generate them. These great circles of earth and stone are repositories of ancient power that focus the energies of the entire landscape and through their celestial alignments, the power of the heavens too. Arbor Low continues to attract and fascinate. In recent years, I have found it occupied with Goddess worshippers lying on the stones to draw on the healing energy. On another occasion, an entire coach load of dowsers was at work trying to calculate the lines of energy. On my last visit, whilst making a video with a couple of my students I was peremptorily told by a lady in black that Arbor Low was a sacred place and I had no right to desecrate it with my camera!

Five Shamanic Landscapes

Arbor Low is one of many monuments that span the Neolithic and the Bronze Ages in this part of the Peak. A few miles from Arbor Low, on a quarried hill known as Stanton Moor, are the remains of a Bronze Age cemetery and ritual landscape. Stanton Moor forms a high platform a couple of miles west of the spa town of Matlock. It is formed out of Gritstone, detached from other high ground by the erosive power of the River Derwent. Odd, sculpted blocks of stone rise out of the thin soil, natural curiosities that must have seemed like the work of gods to people of ancient time. The moor possesses the sad remnants of around seventy Bronze Age cairns as well as five stone circles. I possess a piece of wood from Stanton Moor, picked up on the day of my very first visit. It is a piece of thorn tree, desiccated, weathered, twisted, and looking for all the world like a mummified claw. It reflects the mood of the heath.

This had been the spiritual heart of a people, the burial place of their ancestors, holy ground. Now it is a 'blasted heath', quarried and tortured, its treasures pillaged. Where have the bones, pottery, weaponry and jewels of the dead gone? I recently acquired a first edition of a book by a certain Thomas Bateman, entitled 'Ten Years Diggings in Celtic and Saxon Grave Hills'. The book was published in 1861. Bateman's descriptions of his 'diggings' are instructive. Here he describes the history of a barrow close to Arbor Low:

"On the 15th of March, we re-opened a barrow near the boundary of Middleton Moor, in the direction of Parcelly Hay, which was unsuccessfully opened by Mr. W. Bateman on the 28th July 1824; nor did our researches lead to a more satisfactory result, as the entire mound seemed to have been turned over by deep ploughing by which the internments, consisting of two skeletons and a deposit of burnt bones, had been dragged about as to present no characteristic worthy of observation. A neat whetstone was picked up amongst the ruins, and a carefully chipped leaf-shaped arrow-point of flint has since been found by ploughing across the barrow."[27]

Bateman was one of hundreds of gentlemen who dug barrows as a leisurely pursuit. He and others destroyed what had survived four or five millennia in an afternoon, taking away trinkets, bits of bronze and any pot that would stand the lifting, leaving the rest to the elements. The nineteenth century witnessed an orgy of barrow digging, which ripped the heart out of many of our sacred landscapes. Bateman himself butchered an estimated 187 barrows. He at least recorded his finds and in some instances has left us plans and sections of his excavations. Nonetheless, he rarely took more than a day to dig a barrow and once attempted to dig four in one day.[28]

Stanton Moor's one surviving stone circle is a popular destination for walkers. However neglected or forgotten the many broken cairns on the moor may be, the 'Nine Ladies' stone circle has a steady stream of visitors. Throughout the

Five Shamanic Landscapes

summer people camp there, searching for that special experience that only stone circles can provide. On a recent visit I found a group of children were camped at the circle. A child sat on each of the stones, like fairies sat on mushrooms, whilst an adult told them that the stones were witches, petrified for dancing on the Sabbath. Gone, but not forgotten.

My favourite walk in this part of the world begins and ends in the shadow of this sad remnant of the Bronze Age and it is this journey I would like to share with you now.

The walk is short and straightforward enough to be undertaken on a summer's evening, or in the teeth of the winter snow. It follows ancient paths that link the villages of these parts – Birchover, Youlgreave, Alport and Stanton in Peak that all lie within the shadow of the moor. I can visit the remains of five circles and a number of cairns, as well as locales that I feel were of significance long before the circles were raised.

My path begins at the 'Red Lion Inn' in the village of Birchover. Birchover lies in the shadow of Stanton Moor and a walk of a few minutes brings me to the ruined cairns and stone circles that once dominated this high and lonely place. Like many villages in this part of the Peak, Birchover is unspoilt, thanks to being in a National Park with the building restrictions this implies. From one end of the village to the other is a treat of quaint cottages, with beautiful cottage gardens. At the bottom of the village, where the road curves sharply to the right, there is the aptly named, 'Druid Inn'. The path leaves the road and follows the lane to the left of the inn toward the Parish Church of St. Michael and All Angels. The name of the church is also significant, reflecting the desire to keep the old demons at bay. The need to do this must have been felt more acutely in the superstitious age when the church was built. At the bottom of the lane, with its magnificent old church and vicarage, is a spring, and an usual rock outcrop. Given its relationship to Stanton Moor I have no doubt that this locale would have been a sacred place in ancient times.

At the spring we meet open countryside and a path through grass, bracken and mixed deciduous woodland leads steadily upwards to one of the areas most notable natural curiosities. The landmark is known as 'Robin Hood's Stride'. Robin Hood's stride is a huge block of gritstone. Situated about thirty metres apart on top of this block are two columns of stone. The 'stride' between the two rocks, needless to say, could not be made without magical powers. Close by, set into another rocky outcrop used by climbers is another ancient site known simply as the 'Hermit's Cave'. The rocks above the 'Hermit's Cave' have curious grooves worn into the top edges, where more than half of a century of climbers' ropes have scarred the soft stone.

Five Shamanic Landscapes

The existence of this ancient cave is enough in itself to attract the practitioner of the magic arts. Caves have always been regarded as entrances to the otherworld and remain so in historical memory. Likewise 'Robin Hood's Stride' is so distinctive that it would be odd indeed if our Bronze Age forbears had not found the rock pillars as much a curiosity as we do today. The association with Robin Hood – one of the aliases of the Green Man - is our first clue. The near and intervisible Stone Circle at Harthill Farm provides further evidence, as does the shattered remnants of a prehistoric fortification built on the ground above the Hermit's Cave. Ancient monuments are never random in their siting. Always, some mystery of Nature has created that setting out of which the numen is generated. We may imagine, with some justification that the two great pillars of stone and the nearby cave permitted journeys both inward and outward – to the world above the earth and the world beneath. Perhaps shamans would demonstrate their powers of flight by leaping effortlessly from one stone to the other. In the eye of the believer, that impossible feat had been attained, for in those days shamans flew through the sky for real and not just in the imagination.

There may be little by way of archaeological evidence to support my shamanic whimsy, although the building of two large, ancient earthworks, a stone circle and a standing stone in the immediate vicinity are proof enough that our forbears regarded this place to be of special significance. That communities have dwelt here over the millennia is certain. That they could have ignored these unique rock formations in their quest to penetrate the 'mystery of things' seems unlikely. The so-called Hermit's Cave is not so much a cave as a deep depression in the rock, providing good shelter, but not leading into the bowels of the earth. Nonetheless, its presence seems to have been noted since ancient times. Such grottos are used the world over by shamans as their nexus with the otherworld and we can only speculate that it might have been used as such in the days of the Bronze Age.

The path from Robin Hood's Stride now cuts a diagonal across two fields to the road. This flattish area of fertile arable land is known as Harthill. Moor. To the right, as you walk across the field's to the road, the stone circle, known as 'Nine Stone Close' comes into view. This is the only circle in the Peak constructed of large standing stones. Sadly, only four stones survive, each over six feet tall. John Barnatt, in his book, 'Stone Circles of the Peak'[29], makes much of the alignments of these stones with the pillars of 'Robin Hood's Stride.' His wonderful book still provides the best gazetteer of stone circles in the Peak and first edition hardbacks are sought after. Barnatt discusses the geometrical complexities and alignments of the stone circles, as if the builders of these circles watched and plotted endlessly before constructing these circles with the precision of modern surveyors. This time, however, it would be churlish to doubt that the natural alignments of Robin Hood's Stride inspired this neighbouring circle.

Five Shamanic Landscapes

Remains of 'Nine Stones Close', Harthill Moor

The Limestone Way, one of the Peak's great walking routes can be joined here. It now runs below Harthill Farm along a footpath running through a wood below the Castle Ring. Castle Ring is itself a prehistoric monument, dating pack to the heroic age of the Celts. Walls and a farm track now make it difficult to appreciate the remains of this earthwork. It provides evidence that this densely settled Bronze Age landscape, remained populace in the time of the Celts, when Druids carried out new rituals in their famous groves. The wood below Castle Ring is a fine mixed wood that winds gently round the hill. The path leaves the wood and then follows the Limestone Way toward Youlgreave. Following the tradition of all ghost roads, the path aims for the church tower at the heart of the village. Ever present is the high ground of Stanton Moor to the East. Crowned with its blanket of purple heather, the moor watches over the land of the living. Against darkening skies the villagers of the Bronze Age could have watched the funeral pyres atop the moor illumine the sky. It is a perfect location for a Hill of the Dead.

Not far from Youlgreave rises the River Bradford. It is crossed by a pretty stone bridge, which joins a footpath to the nearby village of Alport. This is a fine and beautiful path, with a limestone outcrop to the right and the stream to the left. It is much used by walkers at weekends. Sacred pathways are defined by streams and rivers and this is probably a very ancient path indeed, coming from the steep sided valley in which the River Bradford rises and following its journey to its confluence with the River Wye, a couple of miles away. The path follows the river to Alport, where magnificent flagstone-roofed cottages decorate the lanes. The cottages, with their beautifully kept gardens, built on a curious twist of narrow lanes canopied by ancient trees, conspire to create a scene that would have inspired William Morris. At Alport, I depart the stream, for it is time to head for the Moor. Stanton in Peak is a little over two miles along green paths and narrow country lanes.

Stanton-in-Peak is a fine old village, with all the features of a bygone age, including its grand manor house. The narrow, winding lanes, rise steeply towards the moor, from whose quarried flanks most of the houses were built. The village has

Five Shamanic Landscapes

an interesting pub, with the curious name of the 'Flying Childers Inn'. (I won't resist the temptation of suggesting it might be something to do with the offspring of shamans!). The fine old parish church of the Holy Trinity lies at the heart of the village and is passed as you follow the road through the village and take the lane to Lees Cross Quarry and Stanton Moor. The Moor has been quarried since time immemorial and its ancient monuments have not saved it from continuing spoilation. There are several working quarries to this day.

Bound by the roads from Birchover to Stanton-in-Peak and Stanton Lees, the moor occupies an area of about a hundred and fifty acres. Over seventy cairns have been identified, although the casual observer could be forgiven for not noticing any of them. Few are obvious to the untutored eye. Those that can be seen are largely ruined and shapeless, and you need to know where to look to find them. This is not a place of spectacle but of memory. The OS 1:25000 map now shows a mere three cairns, and this is perhaps the best guide to what can easily be found. I have located several others as I have wandered the moor, but it is one of the curiosities of the place that what you find one week you cannot locate the next.

In late summer, Stanton Moor has an almost complete covering of purple heather – an astonishing sight, and I have not seen the like anywhere south of the Scottish border. It is the only hilltop in the entire Peak with this covering, a consequence of the absence of sheep. The heather looks like a giant purple pall draped over the remains of our Bronze Age forbears. Man may have destroyed what was once here, but nature has not forgotten. Buried deep, root-wrapped, the bones still feed the heather and the graceful silver birch.

As well as the cairns, three henge monuments survive as low, heather covered rings of rubble of between forty and eighty feet in diameter. The best preserved lies close to the Nine Ladies Stone Circle, a little south of the birch copse in which the circle stands. Few notice the monument, which was probably once of greater significance than the stone circle. Solitude can be found here, once evening falls, and the mood is starker and more demanding of the soul than the cosy familiarity of the Nine Ladies. The glimmer of a fire or distant laughter from the regular visitors to the Nine Ladies may disturb the ghosts in summer, but in the stark autumnal nights, the grip of the otherworld is strong.

Unlike the familiar linear cemeteries of Stonehenge, the Dorset Ridgeway or Kilmartin Glen, the barrows of Stanton Moor are scattered or grouped in clusters. Ashbee defines barrow groupings as 'linear, nuclear and dispersed'.[30] The nuclear groupings are usually clustered around a central barrow, possibly a 'founder' barrow that is older than the rest. At Stanton Moor, the flat hill top itself seems to provide the focus as there is no specific evidence of a 'founder' monument. The two major henge monuments on Stanton Moor and the Nine

Five Shamanic Landscapes

Ladies Stone Circle are curious in that they are isolated from the greater concentrations of barrows. It is possible that the henges are earlier, in that they conform to a pattern we associate with the later Neolithic. I have been unable, however, to find any information that would date the henges to an earlier period than the Bronze Age Cairns. It would seem, therefore, that this cemetery represents the monuments of a single age. Ashbee argues that barrow cemeteries were often built on agricultural land, close to centres of habitation.[31] Given the number of cairns it is possible that Stanton Moor served a number of tribal communities. How or why Stanton Moor was selected will probably remain a mystery, but there are some possibilities. John Barnatt argues for a complex geometrical alignment with the great Neolithic henge monuments at Arbor Low and Dove Holes, but, in the absence of any intervisibility, I find his argument unconvincing.[32]

Another possibility is that the natural stone formations found on Stanton Moor provided the focus for a ritual landscape. As with Robin Hood's Stride, Stanton Moor possesses some unusual stone outcrops, such as the Cork Stone and the Andle Stone. Unusual rock outcrops the world over have spiritual associations – instance Ayres Rock in Australia or 'the grotto' in Lourdes. Can it be a coincidence that three of the most prominent stone circles in the area are associated with unusual rock outcrops? Natural phenomena, both of the earth and the sky are, I believe, the key to understanding the positioning of ritual monuments in the Neolithic and Bronze Ages. This same patterning is observable in Anglesey, where unusual rock outcrops attracted the building of several tombs, such as the passage grave of Bryn Celli Dhu with its associated dome of natural rock.

On the other side of the Birchover Road is the Andle Stone, a huge cube of a rock that can be climbed using iron hoops cemented into the rock. Above it, in a secluded wood is another stone circle – the Doll Tor stone circle. This powerful and atmospheric place is less well known and harder to find than the Nine Ladies. In all my visits, I have had the circle to myself. None other than Thomas Bateman plundered the cairns surrounding the Doll Tor circle. His little book provides both a description of the circle and an account of his act of destruction:

On" the 10th of April, 1852, in company with Mr. Carrington, and Mr. Glover, the Historian of the County of Derby, I walked over a considerable part of Stanton Moor, in order to survey the scene of former discoveries, and to examine the existing remains of Tumuli, Rocking Stones, &c., upon this interesting tract of land. On passing over the brow of the hill, near the Andle Stone, we noticed a small circle of six stones, four of which retained their upright position, whilst two were prostrate, the diameter being about twenty feet; in the interior were a few small pieces of pottery, and some calcined

Five Shamanic Landscapes

bones that had been scratched up by rabbits, the sight of which caused us to set to work with our pocket knives, when finding the remains to become more plentiful, we borrowed a hack and spade from the adjoining farm, and cleared a considerable space in the centre of the enclosure, where a grave had been dug for the reception of three or four cinerary urns, and as many 'incense cups'; all of which had been emptied of their calcined contents, and broken by former diggers, who, however, left the fragments."[33]

Despite so much vandalism, the circle survives, and the two fallen stones are now restored to their sockets – although two of the stones were mysteriously shattered during the restoration process. Thankfully, they too were restored. As well as the remains of four burials found by Bateman, five more burials were found in the 1930s, three of them close to the stones of the main circle. Now set within a copse, with far reaching views, it is a magical place. It is a tribute to the powerful spirits of place that protect this circle that it has survived such an onslaught and still stands, as it has done for over three thousand years.

Stone circle, Doll Tor, Stanton Moor

The physical evidence of the Peak District's Bronze Age may be mutilated, but the dead are not moved from their resting place quite so easily. Whether their spirits reside under the earth or in the sky, the nexus of our meeting remains the place where they were laid to rest. Their spirits are still palpable in this strange, haunted landscape. For the shamanic practitioner, the Peak provides an elemental harshness and a sense of isolation, which requires psychic toughness if you are to spend the night on the misty moor, in the dark copses or amongst the burial places of the long dead. For all that, it is embedded in my own past and I am rooted to it. When I am dead, I too will be a part of this landscape and those that follow will sense my presence as a tingling of the spine in the dead watches of the night.

Shamanism and Sacred Landscapes

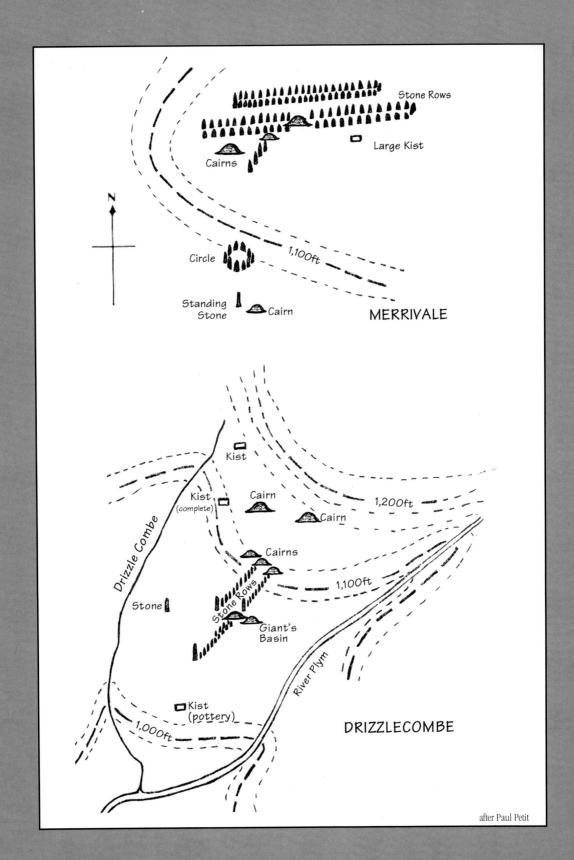

Shamanism and Sacred Landscapes

Five Shamanic Landscapes

4.5. The Twilight of the Shaman
Dartmoor

Dartmoor lies in the South West of Britain and consists of over two hundred square miles of pasture, open heath, blanket peat bog and hills crowned with weather-sculpted towers of granite, known as tors. Parts of the moor are in excess of 1600 feet above sea level, making the high ground a cold and exposed landscape for much of the year. The great granite slab that is Dartmoor is scarred with a multitude of valleys, whose rivers and streams carry off the heavy rainfall that the moor endures. Today, the high moor is thinly populated, with modern-day settlement largely confined to the lower, more fertile ground on the edges of the moor. The exception is the town of Princeton, which has grown up around the grim and forbidding Victorian prison, built in the heart of Dartmoor because the harshness of the climate and inhospitable landscape added to the difficulty of escape. Those who have read Conan Doyle's 'Hound of the Baskervilles' will know what I'm talking about.

Dartmoor has many moods. Sometimes it wraps itself in such deep mist that you cannot see the ground at your feet. Often, it is so rainswept that once friendly paths become an engulfing morass. And sometimes it bakes under a summer sun and the endless day can be spent wandering beneath the granite tors that rise in all their ruggedness to meet the azure skies. In all its moods it practices to deceive. The fool who goes abroad without map, compass and waterproofs risks death in a land where the mist can grow from the earth in moments. Two hundred square miles of mist and morass is a lot to get lost in and many a walker has rued the day they set off ill-prepared.

It is a desolate landscape, and in its desolation lies its beauty. Despite its apparent wildness, the hand of man is everywhere apparent on the moor. There are the remains of thousands of prehistoric dwellings here, dating back to the late Bronze Age and early Iron Age. Their survival speaks of Dartmoor's long desertion and the impact that the people of that distant era had on the landscape.

It is a popular belief that our distant ancestors provide the model of how to live in harmony with the natural environment. The evidence supports the belief to a point. We tend to forget, however, that survival in those distant times was often a harsh and bloody struggle. Nature can be bountiful – but she can also be cruel. Since the Neolithic Revolution, when man took up the plough and the polished axe, he has sought to contend with Nature and to bend Her will to his. Sometimes the outcome has been a garden of peerless beauty – and sometimes man has left the earth a sterile and exhausted wilderness.

Five Shamanic Landscapes

As hunter-gatherers of the Old Stone Age, humans had burnt clearings in the forests to create glades where animals would come to graze. In those days, small-scale 'slash and burn' economies encouraged bio-diversity. The clearings created opportunities for a range of plants to thrive, as well as the animals that fed on them. The forest regenerated with time. In the early Neolithic, we learnt to coppice trees, creating woodland with a thin tree canopy that encouraged a veritable explosion of flora and fauna. Human ingenuity almost seemed a part of Nature's plan. As the Neolithic grew to maturity, however, and the creation of rich pasture and arable land encouraged population growth, that harmonious relationship began to sour. Old fairy tales from Europe are revealing because they show the antipathy that developed between man and the forest. No longer a resource that satisfied all our needs, forests became dark and dangerous places, where lurked evils both natural and supernatural. It became the abode of the witch and the wolf. So the axe fell and fires blazed, as they still do in rainforests around the world. Blindly, we wreaked havoc on that which once gave us life. It was the shaman's habitat too, and the killing of trees has become a symbol of the psychic rupture between man and the natural world.

Around four thousand years ago, the technological know-how to make axes of bronze reached Britain. The large numbers of axe-hoards that have been found in Britain prove that the axe was the most prolifically used tool. This leap in technology was to speed up a process that had already begun – the destruction of Britain's forests and woodlands. At the start of the Bronze Age, Britain was still largely forested. The effect of Bronze Age forest and woodland clearance on Britain's uplands helped to induce local soil deterioration and blanket peat formation.[34] Evidence of serious environmental degradation is apparent in parts of the Lake District, particularly around the Neolithic 'axe factories' on the slopes of the Langdales. In the Langdales the industry that had grown around the manufacture of stone axes created a population pressure that resulted in the wholesale destruction of local forests. Where eco-systems were fragile, as with many of Britain's uplands, they have never recovered.

The basic farming economy of Bronze Age Dartmoor moved from pig grazing to the rearing of cattle and sheep. The 'new' technology of well-made and efficient bronze axes was used to clear away the oak woodlands. At the same time, cereal cultivation became a significant aspect of Dartmoor's economy. The evidence for the increased growing of cereals has been found in the form of cereal pollen dating back to this period as well as the occasional find of the remains of stone querns for grinding the cereal grains into flour[35]. The result of the intensification of farming was the deterioration of the moor into heath, and the formation of blanket peat and bog in wetter and more exposed areas. The deterioration had begun early in the Bronze Age and Blanket Peat was already starting to form over north central Dartmoor. A cooling in the climate towards the end of the Bronze Age meant that this already impoverished land could no

Five Shamanic Landscapes

longer sustain an agrarian population of any size. Farming moved to lower ground, leaving the high moor de-populated, except for the tin mines and some light summer grazing.[36]

The de-population of Dartmoor meant that a wealth of domestic settlements from prehistoric times has survived. Over two thousand buildings and several hundred tombs can still be identified. The greatest concentrations lie in the south-facing valleys. These settlements, known locally as 'pounds', consist of a number of hut circles surrounded by a stone wall, some of which survive to their full height. These were not fortifications, but the homes of herdsmen, and the walls would have enabled them to corral their animals to prevent them being predated or stolen[37]. Larger, open settlements, referred to as villages, have also survived. There are literally hundreds of these settlements across the moor. In keeping with typical Bronze Age architecture, the majority of the dwellings are circular, built of earth banks and dry-stone walling. Excavation has shown that they would have had a conical roof of turf, with a central pole supporting rafters of timber.

As well as the wealth of evidence of domestic life in Bronze Age Britain that has survived on the moor it also has several hundred burial cairns from the Early Bronze Age. These cairns are usually quite small, little more than thirty or forty feet across, attesting to the early and more primitive times in which they were built. They conceal either small burial pits or stone-lined cists. Some of the cists were large enough to contain a crouched inhumation. Others were only large enough to contain the burnt bones of a cremation.

Many of the burial cairns are a part of ritual landscapes that Paul Pettit, in his book on Dartmoor, refers to as 'sanctuaries'. Typically, long rows of standing stones were constructed, which guide the footsteps towards the cairn. These stone rows are often hundreds of metres long. They may be a single, double or triple even row. On Dartmoor there are about sixty known examples of single, double or multiple rows of stones focussed on cairns.[38] These rows are generally constructed out of small stones, perhaps two or three feet high. Much larger monoliths are often incorporated at the terminals of the stone rows. These terminal stones seem to have been selected for their unusual or symmetrical form. This simple 'architecture' reflects religious beliefs that are still focussed on the worship of ancestors. It demonstrates the survival of the belief system that we associate with shamanism – a belief in the power and importance of ancestor spirits.

Why do I see all of this as evidence of the twilight of the shamans?

Drizzlecombe, one of the ritual landscapes I will be describing later in the chapter, provides part of the answer. Encroaching on the cairns that are the focus of this sacred landscape are the remains of a settlement site. The remains

Five Shamanic Landscapes

of the settlement now dominate the crown of the hill. In effect, the hut circles of the living have slighted the great cairns of the dead. This would seem to indicate that the religious beliefs of the cairn builders had passed from memory. In the dying days of the Bronze Age and the coming of Iron, the world was changing. The symbiosis of man and Nature, in which the shaman is the intermediary par excellence, had fractured in this now desolate landscape.

Long centuries have passed since the bitter, acid soil of Dartmoor dissolved the bones of the people who farmed these lands. But the monuments survive, as do the spirits of those who made them. The ritual landscapes were designed to create an experience – a journey from the middle world of the living to the dark and closed world of the dead. The isolation of the moor offers an opportunity to experience the mood of those distant times. There are dozens of sacred sites on Dartmoor, all of them evocative in their own distinctive way. Mindful, however, of the often unforgiving nature of the Dartmoor climate I offer the reader two sacred locales that are relatively safe to access, regardless of the seasons.

Merrivale.

Merrivale lies just a few hundred metres from the B3357 that runs across the moor from Tavistock towards Princeton and its grim prison. Busy in season and good weather, the road has a forsaken feeling in winter, when the cloud descends and little can be seen beyond the 30 metres of road in front of you. Merrivale offers good parking. Shortly after Merrivale quarry a roadside sheep pen of stone rubble has been modified to provide a sheltered car park. Running from the back of the car park is a leat or small watercourse, which can be followed all the way to the impressive stone rows of Merrivale. The leat runs between the stone rows. This is a man-made watercourse, constructed in the nineteenth century, and should be ignored in considering the symbolism of the monument. Until recently, the leat was badly maintained and often turned the area between the stone rows into a morass. Thankfully, it has been restored and tends to stay within its banks for much of the year. If you are not a historical purist, its presence seems fitting. Watercourses often attract ancient monuments. In this instance, the ancient monument has attracted a watercourse.

The choice of setting for these impressive stone rows, stone circle and cairns is clearly deliberate. The builders of this monumental landscape chose the only piece of level ground for miles around. It is encircled by the granite crowned tors that ring the area like abstract gargoyles. Merrivale has the feeling of an arena. The ground slopes away to all sides of the plateau, giving the locale prominence within the general landscape and providing wide-ranging views in all directions. And yet, the monuments themselves are unassuming. Natural forces have littered the ground with stones of a similar size to those used in the stone rows. The site proclaims two stone rows, unique on Dartmoor in that they

Five Shamanic Landscapes

are both double rows for their entire length. The two rows are virtually parallel, and the slight degree of error means that they were intended to focus on the same direction. The space between the pairs of stone varies but is certainly wide enough to walk through. Thus the rows provide a directed experience, just as the cursus does, but to what end? Stone rows usually have some kind of a focus – a cairn or cist, or a large standing stone.

Several cairns occupy the plateau. Only one, however, appears to have a specific relationship with the stone rows. One cairn sits astride the longer southern stone row. Beneath the southern row, however, are the remains of a very substantial cist – built on almost megalithic proportions. The covering slab now lies in two pieces – split in two by a mason's drill and then abandoned. Originally it must have weighed three or four tons. The slabs that construct the walls of the cist are also substantial. The western wall consists of a single, monumental slab of around six by three feet. Substantial, squared off slabs occupy the eastern wall and the end. Clearly the tomb belonged to a significant individual and we may assume a substantial cairn once covered the tomb.

Double stone row, Merrivale

Below the southern terminus of the stone rows is a fascinating group of monuments consisting of a fine stone circle, with eleven surviving stones. It is a neat, almost perfect circle. Close by is a cairn, flanked by what was once two fine standing stones. One, about nine feet high, stands to the west of the cairn. A second stone, now fallen, lies to the east. Other small stones have been erected close by, undoubtedly offering a meaning and a symbolism that is now lost to us. The circle, cairn and standing stones appear to form a ritual grouping in their own right, and seem independent of the stone rows. The only possibility for a link lies with the positioning of a further cairn, towards the western end of the southern row, which has a short stone row extending from it aiming in the general direction of the stone circle. Was it intended to join up with this monument? The southern row also provides some evidence that it has been extended, in that larger stones interrupt both rows at this point. The sanctuary at Merrivale appears to have been constructed piecemeal and our interpretation of the monument must lie in understanding its individual components.

Shamanism and Sacred Landscapes

Five Shamanic Landscapes

At the eastern end of the stone rows a line of cairns also strikes off southwards. These cairns appear to straddle a wall and given their ruinous state we may safely assume that the wall was partly built from stones robbed from the cairns.

Shortly after the cist on the double southern row, you find a cairn interposed on the double stone row. The cairn has been plundered. There seems to be a small central cist at the heart of the barrow, only large enough, in this instance, to receive the ashes of the dead and perhaps a small cremation urn or a beaker. Without excavation it is impossible to tell if the stone row was created to align on the barrow or the barrow deliberately built on this focal point.

The stone rows are constructed of pairs of stones. Little can be interpreted from the chosen shapes. They appear, with the exception of the terminus stones, to have no particular gradation of sizes and some of the stones are very small indeed. Given how little is known of these sites – there has been little by way of modern surveying and what excavation has taken place is old and piecemeal. In this instance, as with all such monuments on the moor, it is safer to interpret such monuments in the generality, drawing from what they have in common.

Nonetheless, the rows at Merrivale appear in a remarkable state of preservation, although we may conjecture that cairns on which these rows once aligned, have been robbed away.

The ceremonial area itself is substantially free of ancient settlement, although the remains of hut circles are scattered across the landscape to the immediate north of the stone rows. The hut circles overlook both the cairns of the ancestral dead and the ritual landscape created by the stone rows and circles.

What is apparent is an integration of tombs and ritual space. This leads to the conclusion that the dead are still the focus of ritual experience in the Early Bronze Age. Although I am arguing for a decline in the practice of shamanism towards the end of the Bronze Age, the use of 'ancestor spirits' to intervene in the affairs of the living has never quite gone away. The clearest example of this is the role of 'saints' in the Roman Catholic Church. Roman Catholics are encouraged to pray to saints. Saints are significant and 'holy' men and women within the Catholic tradition who are deemed to have gone to heaven and hence to be capable of direct communication with God. Hence, they are perceived as acting as intermediaries, pleading on our behalf with the Almighty. The evidence for their status as saints lies in the evidence for miracle wrought in their name.

What is missing in the Roman Catholic Church is an institutional role for the shaman. They survive in the form of the occasional mystic who might be 'transported' into the presence of the Divine, but these are now a rare occurrence in the West (although the generation of altered states of consciousness is still

Five Shamanic Landscapes

apparent in African Christianity and indeed in some evangelical churches). The entombed hero or chieftain is the saint of the Bronze Age. His status or valour has earned him a place amongst the lower echelons of the gods and to him we appeal at times of need.

But what is distinctive about shamanism is its methodology – the harnessing of states of altered consciousness in order to attain that communication with spirits – and demonstrating this remains problematic. The containment of experience through the construction of visual foci may alter how we experience something, but that is not the same as an altered reality. There is a difference between directing experience – as virtually every sacred construction strives to do – and a state of altered consciousness induced by drugs, shamanic drumming or sensory deprivation.

The evidence for shamanism lies in what we can glean from these monuments and their landscapes. Where a community believes in the presence of the dead the relationship with them must be mediated. It is mediated by individuals with the power so to do and it is mediated through the creation of sacred spaces in which movement from the middle world of men to the otherworld of departed souls is symbolically defined for the laity through the construction of monuments. The stone rows and circles define such a journey.

Drizzlecombe.

Drizzlecombe lies on an isolated part of Dartmoor, some 4½ miles east of Yelverton. Narrow lanes of the B3212 take you to the very beautiful Burrator Reservoir and the village of Sheepstor. From Sheepstor a lane can be followed by car towards Ditsworthy Warren. At the end of the lane there is parking for a few cars. The Drizzlecombe stone rows have been described as the most significant group of monuments in Dartmoor. Some of that is down to scale. The site has two of the most impressive cairns and three very large standing stones, including the tallest on Dartmoor. More significant still, is the integrity of the monument, with the stone rows clearly aligned on a triad of cairns. This unity of conception is enhanced by the landscape itself. Drizzlecombe presents as a smooth, convex slope, with watercourses to either side. On the southern side flows the River Plym. On the northern side flows Drizzle Combe, which gives the monument its name. The two form a confluence at the foot of the slope, an indicator of a sacred site in itself.

The best approach to Drizzlecombe (and the safest in poor visibility) is by way of the new track to Ditsworthy Warren House. This track has recently been re-laid with brilliant white gravel and provides a pleasant contemplative walk upward towards Eastern Tor and Drizzle Combe beyond. To the left of the track is Gutter Mire, where dank, stagnant pools remind us of the more sinister

Five Shamanic Landscapes

dimension of the moor. The track leads behind the grim, shuttered and padlocked Ditsworthy Warren House, and skirts Eastern Tor before descending into Drizzle Combe. There is a curious symmetry to Drizzlecombe. The slope of the ground rises evenly, almost gracefully, towards the crest of the hill and the original 'founding' cairn. Drizzle Combe and the River Plym define a triangle of land dominated by ancient cairns and stone rows. The symmetry of the landscape invites symmetry in the work of men and indeed this is the case. A large, ancient cairn dominates the higher ground. Below this cairn, our Bronze Age forbears built a line of three small cairns, forming a triangle with the larger cairn above. Curiously, it is the three relatively small cairns that appear to be the focus of the stone rows and indeed of the entire ritual landscape. Originally, it would seem that three stone rows were planned, each one creating a processional route towards the cairn on which it is aligned.

Double stone row, Drizzlecombe

The largest standing stones are used to form the starting point of each stone row. The southern row is by far the longest, and this has the largest standing stone on Dartmoor part way along its length. I estimated the height at about fourteen feet. It has an almost face-like projection at the top and the stone is orientated so the 'face' looks towards the cairn at the end of the alignment. There is a second cairn on this same alignment and the second section of the stone row is focussed on this cairn. At end of the south row, the very large terminal stone is again orientated so the broader 'face' of the stone is aligned on the cairn at the far end. This stone presents as no more than thirty centimetres thick when viewed at ninety degrees to the stone row. When viewed from the row itself it presents as a large, almost triangular stone, a metre across at the base. What this reveals is a basic 'architecture' of a cairn, usually on higher ground, with a stone row of relatively small stones leading to it, and a larger terminal stone at the end of the row. Most of the terminal stones that I came across appear to have been selected for their size and symmetry, or, in some instances, because of their unusual shape. Situated a little to the SE of this row is another cairn, known as the Giant's Basin. This cairn is aptly named, being the largest of the surviving cairns, although not strictly part of the arrangement of the ritual landscape as a whole. It too, has attracted its own little array of satellite cairns.

Five Shamanic Landscapes

Situated on the crest of the hill that provides the overall focus for the ritual landscape are the walls and hut circles of a settlement. It is not uncommon to find ancient walls and hut circles intruding on the monuments and the general picture seems to be one of a decline of respect for the ancestral tombs. This, in the absence of any dating evidence for the relative ages of tombs and hut circles cannot be proven, but the positioning of the settlements is clearly intrusive on the monuments and therefore might be described as 'slighting' them.

The tallest standing stone on Dartmoor, part of Drizzlecombe stone rows

The third of the cairns that forms the focus of the alignments does not have its own stone row. On plotting a line where the row might have been built, however, I found a single, squarish stone, about three feet high, which may have been placed to mark the terminus of the row that was never built. Why these three cairns should be the focus of this ritual landscape will never be known. What they, and other monuments like them, seem to represent, is a symbolizing of the passage grave, or at least the concept behind their design. In order to communicate with the dead, a specific journey must be followed. It is the same idea as the stone avenues of Avebury or the cursus monument at Stonehenge. It is the physical realization of a journey of the soul.

In the late Bronze Age the semi-nomadic lifestyles of the general population finally gave way to settled farming communities, based on farmsteads and small villages. Dartmoor offers powerful evidence of a transition of lifestyle and beliefs that brought an end to half a million years of living in accordance with Nature's laws. With the building of settlements in such a way as to encroach upon the monuments, we also see a decline in respect for ancestral spirits and the spirit of things generally. The decline of the hunter-gatherer lifestyle and the rupture of our relationship with the natural environment marks the beginning of the end for the shaman.[39]

Shamanism and Sacred Landscapes

References

Part 1: Towards a Philosophy of Shamanism

1. Kund Rasmusen, *Across Arctic America* (G.P.Putnam & Sons, 1927)
2. Stephen Larsen, *The Shaman's Doorway*, (Inner Traditions, Rochester, Vermont, 1998) P186
3. Dudley Young, *Origins of the Sacred, The Ecstasies of Love and War*, (Harper Perennial, 1992), P17ff
4. Ibid., P.24
5. Neil del Strother, *The Hawaiian Shaman's Path*, (Kindred Spirit, Autumn 2001) P16
6. Joseph Campbell, *Primitive Mythology – The Masks of God* – (Viking Press 1959, this ed. Penguin Books, 1982) P21-22
7. Mircea Eliade, *Shamanism, Archaic Techniques of Ecstasy*, (Princeton University Press, 1972) P232
8. Carlos Castaneda, *The Teachings of Don Juan: A Yaqui Way of Knowledge* (Arkana, Penguin Books, 1990. Original
   pub. The University of California Press, 1968) P129.
9. William James, *The Gifford Lectures delivered at Edinburgh 1901-2.* (This edition *The Varieties of Religious Experience*, Fount Paperbacks, 1982) P366ff
10. Rudolf Otto, *The Idea of the Holy*, (Oxford University Press, 1923) P7
11. Ibid., P7
12. William James, 1901-2, P377
13. St. John of the Cross, *The Dark Night of the Soul*, book ii. Ch. xvii, quoted in William James 1901-2, P393
14. Friedrich Nietzsche, *Thus Spoke Zarathustra*, (first pub. 1885, trans R.J.Hollinrake, this edition Penguin Books, 1969) P297
15. Paul Devereux, Shamanism and the Mystery Lines, (Quantum 1992)
16. Robert Ackerman, *J.G.Frazer – His Life and Work*, (Cambridge University Press, Canto edition, 1990) P80

References

Part 2: Shamanism and Sacred Landscapes

1. Teilhard de Chardin, *The Phenomenon of Man* (Collins, 1965) P213-214
2. Christopher Tilley, *A Phenomenology of Landscape, Places, Paths and Monuments*, (Berg, Oxford/Providence USA, 1994) P38
3. Ibid., P40-53
4. C.G.Jung, *Alchemical Studies*, (Routledge & Kegan Paul, 1967) P8
5. Carlos Castaneda, 1990, P31
6. Christopher Tilley, 1994, P18
7. Conor Newman, *Tara, An archaeological survey*, (Discovery Programme, Monograph 2, Irish Royal Academy, 1997)
8. Christopher Tilley, 1994, P21
9. Mark Brennand and Maisie Taylor, *Seahenge* (Current Archaeology No167, March 2000) P417-424
10. English Heritage news release, 15th October 2001, (quoted in Third Stone, Issue 41, Winter 2001-2) P2
11. Mike Pitts, *Seahenge Revisited*, (Current Archaeology' No.174, June 2001) P245
12. Rogan Taylor, *The Death and Resurrection Show*, (Anthony Blond, London, 1985) P14
13. Marie-Louise von Franz, *C.G.Jung, His Myth in Our Time*, (C.G. Jung Foundation for Analytical Psychology, 1975) P119
14. Ibid., P112
15. Ibid., P112-113)
16. C.G.Jung, *Alchemical Studies*, P16-17
17. Nevill Drury, *The Elements of Shamanism*, (Element Books, 1989) P99
18. C.G.Jung, *Memories, Dreams, Reflections*, (recorded by Aniela Jaffe, Collins and Routledge & Kegan Paul, London 1963) P176)
19. Marie-Louise von Franz, 1975, P109-110
20. C.G.Jung, *Memories, Dreams, Reflections*, P179)
21. Ibid., P183
22. Ibid., P171
23. Ibid., P183-4
24. Stephen Larsen, *The Shaman's Doorway*, P52-53
25. Knud Rasmussen, *Across Arctic America, Narrative of the Fifth Thule Expedition*, (Copenhagen, 1925) reprinted in Joan Halifax, Shamanic Voices. Pelican Books, 1980
26. Mircea Eliade, 1964, P58-59

References

Part 3:. Interpreting Shamanic Landscapes

1. Stefan Bergh, *Landscape of the Monuments – A study of the passage tombs in the Cuil Irra region.* (Doctoral Dissertation 1995, Dept. of Archaeology, University of Stockholm.) P152
2. Piers Vitebsky, *The Shaman*, (Little, Brown and Company, 1995), P155-6
3. Rudolf Otto, *The Idea of the Holy*, P68
4. Richard Bradley, *Altering the Earth*, (The Rhind Lectures, Society of Antiquaries of Scotland, Monograph Series Number 8, Edinburgh 1993), P2
5. Lloyd and Jennifer Laing, *The Origins of Britain*, (Paladin, 1982), P87
6. Paul Ashbee, *The Fussell's Lodge Long Barrow*, (*Archaeologia*, The Society of Antiquaries, 1966) P45ff and Paul Ashbee, *The Earthen Long Barrow in Britain*, (University of Toronto Press, 1970) P85ff
7. J.G.D. Clark, *Excavations at Star Carr, An early Mesolithic site at Seamer near Scarborough, Yorkshire*, (Cambridge University Press, 1954 & 1971)
8. Ibid., P168ff
9. Ibid., P168ff
10. Mircea Eliade, *Shamanism, Archaic Techniques of Ecstasy*, P459
11. Ibid., P155
12. Ibid., P461
13. J. David Lewis-Williams, *A Cosmos in Stone, interpreting religion and society through Rock Art*, (Altamira Press, 2002)
14. Peter Jordan, *The materiality of shamanism as a 'world-view': Praxis, artifacts and landscape*, (published in *The Archaeology of Shamanism*, edit Neil Price, Routledge, 2001)
15. Ibid., P91
16. Ibid., P93
17. Ibid., P89
18. Mircea Eliade, *Shamanism, Archaic Techniques of Ecstasy*, P160ff
19. See the calibrated radiocarbon dates in Michael O'Kelly, *Newgrange, Archaeology art and legend*, (Thames & Hudson, 1982), P12
20. See Marija Gimbutas, *The Goddesses and Gods of Old Europe*, (Thames & Hudson, 1982).
21. Paul Ashbee, *The Earthen Long Barrow in Britain*, P88
22. Paul Ashbee, *The Fussell's Lodge Long Barrow Excavation*, p37ff
23. Ian Kinnes, *Non-Megalithic Long Barrows and Allied Structures in the British Neolithic*, (British Museum Occasional Paper 52, 1992), P88ff
24. Mircea Eliade, Shamanism, *Archaic Techniques of Ecstasy*, P62
25. Ibid., P159
26. Ibid., P67ff
27. Ibid., P45
28. Ibid., P82
29. Paul Ashbee, *The Earthen Long Barrow in Britain*, P92
30. Richard Bradley, *Altering the Earth*, P79
31. G.J.Wainwright & I.H.Longworth, *Durrington Walls Excavations 1966-1968*, (The Society of

References

Antiquaries, 1971) P198
32. Richard Bradley, *Altering the Earth*, P83
33. Johnston 1993, P144-145
34. Richard Bradley, *Rock Art and the Prehistory of Atlantic Europe*, (Routledge, 1997) P125
35. Michael O'Kelly, *Newgrange, Archaeology art and legend*, P124
36. Jeremy Dronfield, *Subjective Visual Phenomena in Passage Tomb Art*, (published as a series of papers in 37. Cambridge Archaeological Journal, April 1996)
37. Richard Bradley, *Rock Art and the Prehistory of Atlantic Europe*, P52ff
38. Ibid., P55)
39. See *Current Archaeology*,(issue no 188, October 2003) P333
40. Richard Bradley, *Rock Art and the Prehistory of Atlantic Europe*, P51
41. J. D. Lewis-Williams, *A Cosmos in Stone, Interpreting Religion and Society through Rock Art*, (AltaMira Press, 2002)
42. Ibid., P21
43. J.D Lewis-Williams, *Southern African shamanistic rock art in its social and cognitive contexts*, (*The Archaeology of Shamanism*, edit Neil Price, Routledge, 2001) P17ff
44. Johnston 1993, P144-145
45. Richard Bradley, *Rock Art and the Prehistory of Atlantic Europe*, P.49
46. Ibid., P51
47. J.D. Lewis-Williams, *A Cosmos in Stone*, P142
48. Ibid., P142ff
49. Mircea Eliade, Shamanism, *Archaic Techniques of Ecstasy*, P169
50. Ibid., P123)
51. Aubrey Burl, *Prehistoric Avebury*, (Yale University Press, 1979) P202ff
52. Mircea Eliade, Shamanism, *Archaic Techniques of Ecstasy*, P259
53. Ibid., P265
54. Richard Bradley, *Altering the Earth*, P50
55. Ibid., P62
56. Paul Devereux, *Shamanism and the Mystery Lines*, (Quantum, 1992)
57. Ibid., P220
58. Paul Ashbee, *The Bronze Age Round Barrow in Britain*, (Phoenix House Ltd. 1960) P93
59. Ann Woodward, *British Barrows – A matter of life and death*, (Tempus Publishing Ltd., 2000) P121

References

Part 4: Five Shamanic Landscapes

1. For a thorough and well researched summary of the debate see Rodney Castledon, New views across an old landscape: Reassessing Stonehenge, (3rd Stone, Issue 35, July 1999) and *The epic of the Stonehenge Bluestones – Were they moved by ice, or by people?* (3rd Stone, Issue 39, Winter 2000/2001) For the argument in favour of glacial movement of the bluestones see Aubrey Burl, *Myth Conceptions*, (3rd Stone, Issue 37, January 2000)
2. source: posted on *'Wessex Archaeology'* website 21/06/04
3. Paul Devereux, *Shamanism and the Mystery Lines*, P.143
4. Gaynor Francis, *The First Stonehenge*, (Christopher Davies Ltd., 1986)
5. Christopher Tilley, A Phenomenology of *Landscape*, P83-84
6. J.V.S. Megaw and D.D.A. Simpson, *Introduction to British Prehistory*, Leicester University Press, 1979), P86
7. Christopher Thompson Barker, *The Chambered Tombs of South-West Wales*, (Oxbow Monograph 14, 1992) P68
8. Christopher Tilley, *A Phenomenology of Landscape*, P83-84
9. quoted in Christopher Thompson Barker, *The Chambered Tombs of South –West Wales*, P36
10. Ibid., P36
11. See G .J Wainwright and I. H. Longworth, *Durrington Walls, Excavations 1966-1968*, (The Society of Antiquaries, 1971), P202
12. R. J. Mercer, *Causewayed Enclosures*, (Shire Archaeology, 1990) P62
13. For a contemporary description of the destruction see William Stukeley, *Abury, A Temple of the British Druids*, (London, 1743)
14. R. J. Mercer, *Causewayed Enclosures*, P22
15. Richard Jeffries, *Wild Life in a Southern County*, (Smith, Elder, London 1879)
16. G. J. Wainwright and I. H. Longworth, *Durrington Walls*, P191
17. See John W. Hedges, *Tomb of the Eagles*, (Tempus Reparatum, 1984) P133ff
18. see Lloyd & Jennifer Laing, *The Origins of Britain*, (Paladin Grafton Books, 1982)
19. Michael Dames, *The Silbury Treasure, The Great Goddess Rediscovered*, (Thames and Hudson, 1976)
20. Michael Dames, *The Avebury Cycle*, (Thames & Hudson) 1977
21. Mike Pitts, *Collapse at Silbury Hill*, (Current Archaeology, no.176, October 2001) P336ff
22. Aubrey Burl, *Prehistoric Avebury*, (Yale University Press, 1979)P69-70
23. *Kilmartin, Prehistoric & Early Historic Monuments*, (RCAHMS, 1999), P28-29
24. Ibid., P32-33
25. For general reading on Kilmartin's prehistory see *Kilmartin, An Introduction & Guide* by Rachel Butter, photographs David Lyons (pub. Kilmartin House Trust, 1999, available from the Kilmartin House Museum via their website). The excavation and archaeological data for this chapter came from the RCAHMS publication on Kilmartin (see reference 23)
26. Nicholas Thomas, *A Guide to Prehistoric England*, P65 (B.T. Batsford Ltd., 1960)
27. Thomas Bateman, *Ten Years Diggings in Celtic and Saxon Grave Hills, in the Counties of Derby, Stafford and York, from 1848 to 1858*, (J. R. Smith, London, 1861) P24
28. Barry M. Marsden, *The Early Barrow Diggers*, (Shire Publications Ltd, 1974) P39

References

29. John Barnatt, *Stone Circles of the Peak*, (Turnstone Books, London, 1978), P156-158
30. Paul Ashbee, *The Bronze Age Round Barrow in Britain*, P34
31. Ibid., P.37
32. John Barnatt, *Stone Circles of the Peak*, P155
33. Thomas Bateman, *Ten Years Diggings*, P84
34. Ian Simmons and Michael Tooley, *The Environment in British Prehistory*, (Duckworth, 1981), P231
35. Ibid., P243
36. Ibid., P178
37. Paul Pettit, *Prehistoric Dartmoor*, (David & Charles: Newton Abbot, 1974) P.27
38. Paul Ashbee, *The Bronze Age Round Barrow in Britain*, P51
39. Paul Pettit's book, *Prehistoric Dartmoor* provides an excellent summary of Dartmoor's prehistoric monuments. Also see the ever popular R. Hansford Worth, *Dartmoor* (David & Charles, Newton Abbot, 2nd impression, 1971)t